Livana,

What a blessing for me to have you in my life! You are a blessing and I thank God for you.

May God bless you.

Brinn

9-21-17

Strangers to Spouses

Strangers to Spouses

A Study of the Relationship Quality
in Arranged Marriages in India

BINU EDATHUMPARAMBIL

WIPF & STOCK · Eugene, Oregon

Wipf & Stock
An Imprint of Wipf and Stock Publishers
199 W. 8th Ave., Suite 3
Eugene, OR 97401

www.wipfandstock.com

PAPERBACK ISBN: 978-1-5326-1950-2
HARDCOVER ISBN:978-1-4982-4581-4
EBOOK ISBN: 978-1-4982-4580-7

Manufactured in the U.S.A.   AUGUST 21, 2017

Dedicated to my parents,
Aleykutty and Kurian Edathumparambil

Contents

CONTENTS

Part V: Discussion and Interpretation

Figures

Tables

Acknowledgments

As I publish this study, I would like to take a moment to acknowledge and thank those who played a significant role in helping me to accomplish this important milestone in my academic life. The participants of this study are the first people who deserve a special word of thanks. Without their willingness to share their experiences about their marriages and marital relationships, this study would not have been possible. I thank the University of Mysore in India for granting me the permission to conduct this doctoral research in India. I also express my gratitude to all the heads of institutions and communities and other individuals in India who helped me with the recruitment of participants for this study. The faculty, the staff, and my colleagues in the Medical Family Therapy program at Saint Louis University have contributed much to my growth as a clinician and researcher. I express my gratitude to all of them.

I owe a great deal of gratitude to Dr. James Doug Pettinelli, my advisor and chairperson, and the other two committee members, Dr. Eddie M. Clark and Dr. Kristin Wright. They have been a great help in the whole process of the dissertation work. They encouraged me, challenged me, and above all helped me to be passionate about this research work. Sometimes they went out of their way to find the support and resources that I needed. I appreciate all their help. I would also like to acknowledge the support and encouragement that I received from Dr. Lee Smith in the School of Nursing, Dr. Terry Tomazic in the Department of Sociology, and Dr. Kristin Kiddoo in the Department of Psychology at Saint Louis University.

I am grateful to each of the developers of the three instruments that were used in this study—that is, Dr. Susan S. Hendrick for the Relationship

Assessment Scale, Dr. Agnew R. Christopher for the Investment Model Scale, and Dr. Robert J. Sternberg for the Triangular Love Scale. They were prompt in their replies and graciously gave me permission to use and reprint those instruments in this dissertation.

My community, family, and friends have been a great source of support and encouragement in my academic pursuit, particularly during my doctoral studies. I thank all of them.

Introduction

THE INDIAN PENINSULA, SEPARATED from mainland Asia by the Himalayas and surrounded by the Bay of Bengal in the east, the Arabian Sea in the west, and the Indian Ocean in the south, is the largest democracy and the second most populous country in the world today (Carroll, 2009; Guha, 2007). For an outsider, the Indian subcontinent may look like a single cultural unit, but a closer look at the Indian society would reveal to anyone that it is one of the most diversified societies in the world. Home to approximately 1.15 billion people, the diversity of India is prominently visible in its people, culture, climate, language, ethnicity, race, and religion. As Margaret Khalakdina stated, there is "a great deal of heterogeneity" (2008, p. 9) in the Indian society. States and regions are so diverse that people in one state often find it difficult to relate to other Indians in other states because they speak a different language, eat different food, and follow different customs and traditions.

Referring to the complexity in the Indian culture, Nilufer Medora, a professor and researcher in family studies, stated, "India's culture, like its people, is a diverse mosaic whose myriad elements have been born of its ancient history, its foreign influences, urbanization, modernization, and globalization" (2007, p. 167). Other researchers, such as Bandana Purkayastha and her colleagues, also captured this complexity when they said, "It is very difficult to draw a neat boundary around what constitutes 'Indian'" (2003, p. 503). However, the Indian society is like a colorful canvas portraying a picture-perfect assimilation of all these diverse elements and creating a complex amalgam of cultures (Guha, 2007). Describing this unity in diversity, Vijay Joshi, a researcher on India, stated, "To the amazement of many, this vast and complex country has managed to protect national unity, introduce and preserve democracy, and dilute traditional caste hierarchies" (2010, p. 73).

One of the celebrated features of this complex Indian society is its sense of collectivism. Although people speak different languages, dress differently, follow different religions, and eat different food, Indians immensely value social ties and interdependence. A festival or a celebratory event, for example, is never limited to a family or a home. The whole community or neighborhood rises to the occasion and joins the celebration. The collectivistic and interdependent character of the society is seen in the emphasis given to the joint decision-making processes, cooperation between family members, and putting the needs and views of the family above the accomplishment of individual needs and desires (Medora, 2007).

The one institution in which this collectivistic and interdependent character of the society becomes very visible is the institution of marriage. Parents and families in India play an active, and sometimes even an excessive role in the selection of marital partners for their children and making arrangements for their wedding, giving those marriages the unique name, *arranged marriages*. Parents and other responsible adults in families take upon themselves the responsibility of making marital decisions for their children, needing the latter only to consent to the decisions of the former. It is reported that approximately 90 percent of the marriages in India today are arranged marriages (Chawla, 2007; Madathil and Benshoff, 2008; Singh, 2005). Among the Hindus, the majority community in India, this estimate is reported to be even higher, close to 95 percent (Chawla, 2007).

Due to the excessive parental and familial involvement and several other cultural factors, men and women who consent to these arranged marriages often have very limited knowledge of and interaction with their prospective marital partners prior to their marriages. They enter into their marriages basically as strangers, and hence the title of this book, *Strangers to Spouses*.

Given this reality of strangers entering into marital unions without much knowledge about each other, it is not uncommon to hear people, especially in the Western world (e.g., United States), asking the question, "How does that work?" They wonder how couples can live their married lives with so little knowledge about each other prior to their wedding. Several studies have been done on these marriages to see how they work and whether they work at all. The results have been varied and sometimes discrepant. This book is a revised version of a mixed methods study that the author conducted on these marriages as part of his doctoral dissertation. The study looked at the quality of relationship in such marriages in India. Specifically, the study explored the levels of marital satisfaction, quality of alternatives, investment of resources, intimacy, passion, and commitment, and examined their association with relationship quality. The survey of measures was completed by 287 participants. Fourteen of these respondents completed qualitative interviews. The study elicited rich responses from the participants and obtained valuable findings, adding to the knowledge base on such marriages.

The dissertation was published in its original format in 2014 by ProQuest, the Michigan-based electronic publisher of dissertations. A limited version of this study was published as a journal article in 2015 in the *Journal of Behavioral and Social Sciences (Vol. 2, 80–88)*. This book is developed specifically for the purpose of making this research work available to a wider readership. A few changes have been made to the original manuscript. In its original format, the dissertation was divided into five chapters, with chapter headings as Introduction, Literature Review, Methodology, Results, and Discussion. In this revised version, these chapters have been converted into five parts, dividing the content of each part into different chapters so as to make it easier for readers. The content of the book remains the same while the presentation of it has been slightly changed for better and easier readability.

Since the introduction in the original format was turned into Part I of this book, it was thought to be appropriate to provide this short introduction. Part I provides the readers with a general introduction to the whole study. Part II looks at some of the major studies that have been done in the past on marriages across the globe and arranged marriages in India in particular. Part III gives the details about the methodology that was used for the study, which was basically a mixed methods study, consisting of both quantitative and qualitative phases. Part IV presents the findings of the study, both quantitative and qualitative. Those who are unfamiliar with statistics might find it somewhat challenging to understand all the statistical details, but it is the author's hope that the details of the qualitative interviews, especially the quotes and comments from the participants, would balance it out and make the reading of the text more interesting and enjoyable. Part V discusses and interprets the findings of the study, and makes recommendations for future researchers who might want to build on the findings of this study.

PART I

Why This Research?

1

The Research Problem

MARRIAGE IS ONE OF the prime institutions in almost every society across the globe (Coontz, 2005; Musick and Bumpass, 2012). People organize their personal and social lives around the institution of marriage in many societies (Mburugu and Adams, 2005; Singh, 2005). However, cultures and communities differ in the way marriages are conducted and contracted. In some cultures (e.g., United States), matters concerning mate selection and marital life are left to the individuals (Madathil and Benshoff, 2008; Settles, 2005), whereas in others (e.g., India), parents and families are actively involved in choosing a person's marital partner and arranging his or her marriage (Chawla, 2007; Jacobson, 1996). The former is called marriages of choice or love marriages, and the latter is known as arranged marriages.

The majority of marriages in India today are reported to be arranged marriages (Batabyal, 2001; Chawla, 2007). Although the spread of Western values such as individualism and increased social and economic mobility in the past two decades in India have had some influence on people's perception of marriage and mate selection, the majority of Indians still choose the path of arranged marriages rather than marriages of choice (Chawla, 2007; Ganguly-Scrase, 2003).

The current study was aimed at exploring the quality of relationship in arranged marriages in India. This was necessitated by a gap in the current literature, which appeared to present discrepant results regarding this subject. Some studies reported that arranged marriages in India maintained a high persistence rate (no threat of dissolution) and high levels of marital satisfaction (Alexander et al., 2006; Chawla, 2007; Madathil and Benshoff, 2008; Sandhya, 2009). The rate of dissolution of marriages in India was reported to be inconsequential. The 2001 national census put the overall divorce rate in India at 1.1 percent (Batabyal, 2001; Singh, 2005). In the last fifteen years, these findings do not appear to have changed much, except maybe in some urban settings. There is one study (Yelsma and Athappilly, 1988) that showed that arranged marriages in India had higher levels of marital satisfaction than love marriages (marriages of choice) in India and in the United States.

However, these reports and research findings about the low divorce rate and high levels of marital satisfaction did not match with other reports on arranged marriages in India. For example, authors such as Chacko (2003), Medora (2007), Philips (2004), and Singh (2005) found that there were widespread abuses, violence, dowry deaths, humiliation, torture, and lack of freedom in many Indian marriages. These findings raised the question of how reports of high marital satisfaction existed coincidentally with reports of widespread abuses and violence in those marriages. The present study was an effort to better understand these contradictory findings about these marriages by exploring more deeply the nature of relationship quality in those marriages.

The present study utilized a collection of measures utilized in couples research in the West to assess marital quality. These measures were administered in a survey format to individuals who have been wed within the tradition of arranged marriages in India. In addition, a small sample of individuals who had completed the survey were then interviewed about the different dimensions of their marriage. Specifically, the study examined the association of respondents' level of satisfaction, quality of alternatives, investment of resources, intimacy, passion, and commitment with their relationship quality.

THE RESEARCH PROBLEM AND THE NEED FOR THE STUDY IN DETAIL

Among the many collectivistic cultures around the world, India stands out as one of the most diversified and yet close-knit and kinship-oriented societies (Jacobson, 1996; Singh, 2005). Individual members in Indian families are raised to be faithful adherents to the familial and societal expectations. According to Nancy McWilliams, "Deference to authority is a powerfully reinforced norm" in India (2011, pp. 302–3).

Marriage is one of the institutions in India in which this deference to authority and collectivistic nature of the society is very visible. Parents and other family members are actively involved in choosing marital partners for their children and arranging their marriage. In a typical arranged marriage, the bride- and groom-to-be play a passive role in mate selection and marital decisions. Parents or responsible adults in the family arrange marriages "on behalf of and with or without the consent of the boy or the girl" (Singh, 2005, p. 143). The knowledge of potential partners is limited to what is communicated by the intermediary, which often happens to be their own parents or the marriage broker (Philips, 2004). Such culturally approved influence and intervention of parents and families in an individual's life and marital decisions might be viewed as an infringement on one's personal freedom in a country like the United States, where romantic marriages or marriages of choice are more common. In marriages of choice, individual members enter a phase of dating and courtship, and if both partners decide to take their relationship to a permanent commitment as husband and wife, they enter into a marital contract (Myers et al., 2005). The role of parents or family is much less central in such arrangements than it is in arranged marriages.

Although many reasons could exist for these differences between cultures with regard to mate selection and marital practices, authors such as Jane E. Myers and her colleagues (2005) and Yelsma and Athappilly (1988) see it basically as a characteristic arising from the collectivistic or individualistic nature of the society. In collectivistic cultures, the decisions of the family or community get precedence over that of the individual members, whereas in individualistic cultures, the decisions of individual members get precedence over that of the family or community.

Arranged by family or chosen by self, once married, couples pass through different stages in their marital relationship. While some solidify their relationship and persist in their marriage, others escalate in conflicts and break up their relationship. Although the current affairs in the state of marriage across the globe, particularly in the Western world, are reported to be somewhat tumultuous and unpredictable (Gottman, 1999; Hall, 2012; Musick and Bumpass, 2012), there are several studies (Coontz, 2005; Gottman and Gottman, 2008; Hughes, 2007; Rusbult et al., 1998; Sternberg, 1986) that show that there is a high level of satisfaction, stability, and higher functioning in marriages of choice in the West. High rates of divorces and conflicts are real in many marriages of choice in the United States and other

Western countries, but despite all that, many marriages have endured and persisted with a high level of satisfaction (Gottman, 1999).

The arranged marriages in India also report a high level of marital satisfaction and low rate of divorces or separations (Chawla, 2007; Madathil and Benshoff, 2008; Sandhya, 2009; Singh, 2005). People persist in marriage, and families remain united. However, there are reports of very disturbing and negative trends in such marriages. There are reports of widespread abuses, violence, discrimination, and torture against women in such marriages.

Looking into the statistics on abuses and violence in Indian marriages, Singh (2005) found that 40 percent of women in India had experienced violence by an intimate partner. Elaborating on the type of domestic violence, he found that two out of every five married women had reported being hit, kicked, beaten, or slapped by their husbands. About 50 percent of the women who experienced physical violence reported that the abuse took place during pregnancy. Many cases of "wife-battering and forced incest with the women of the household" (p. 153) go unreported. Domestic and sexual violence are rampant but often hidden from public view (Chacko, 2003). Forced incest with the women of the household refer primarily to sexual abuses of daughters by their fathers, nieces by their uncles, and other women in the household by their male relatives or family members (Gopalan, 2009). There are also reports of young people still being pressured to consent to consanguineous marriages (marrying a blood relative or cross-cousin, cross-uncle/niece marriages; Philips, 2004; Singh, 2005). Not wanting to hurt the family ties and other attachment bonds, many of them abide by the decisions of their parents or extended families.

Although giving, taking, and demanding dowry is forbidden in India, many women and their families still bear the brunt of this burdensome practice in many parts of the country (Chacko, 2003; Medora, 2007; Philips, 2004; Shukla, 2009; Singh, 2005). Extreme cases of dowry demands lead to harassment, abuse, and even murder of women in families (Chacko, 2003; Singh, 2005). The dowry system pushes many families to the brink of poverty and burdensome financial commitments (Chacko, 2003; Singh, 2005). Even if they are aware that their married daughters are in unhappy and abusive marriages, many parents are reluctant to allow them to return home for fear of having to pay a second dowry. And if they return home and decide to stay single or unmarried for fear of further abuse they might be considered a burden and shame for the family.

Singh (2005) reported that there were 4,148 dowry deaths in India in 1990. Chacko (2003) cited an example of three sisters in the state of Kerala committing suicide to save their parents from the pain and agony of finding sufficient funds for their dowries and weddings. The largely skewed power difference in favor of males in the family and the overarching influence of the extended families on couples' day-to-day affairs are other factors that characterize couples' relationships in India (Bose and South, 2003; Chekki, 1988; Jacobson, 1996; Singh, 2005). Although the low divorce rate is not to be minimized by any means, there are reports that the prevalence of the social stigma attached to divorce and the consequent isolation and shame for the individuals and families directly or indirectly influence the high persistence rate in such marriages (Bose and South, 2003; Dupree et al., 2013; Medora, 2007; Singh, 2005).

Besides the reports of violence and abuses, the excessive influence of families on marital decisions adds to the complexity and convolution of relationship in arranged marriages in India. Mate selection, as mentioned above, is a societal and familial endeavor, and anything contrary to this expectation might be construed as disloyalty and disobedience. The experience and wisdom of parents and elders are often pitted against the ignorance and lack of experience of the young bride-and groom-to-be in justifying the overarching influence of families in mate selection and marital decisions (Batabyal, 2001; Philips, 2004). Strict submissiveness and deference to the authority of parents and elders are demanded of all the dependents, including the marriage-aged children in the family (Singh, 2005). However, one of the negative consequences of blind adherence to such expectations is that the majority of brides and grooms are undeniably limited in their knowledge of their prospective partners (Alexander et al., 2006; Singh, 2005). They contract their marriages with the minimal information they are given about their prospective brides or grooms (Philips, 2004).

In most cases, the prospective brides and grooms would meet only once before their wedding or engagement, and that often happens during the "bride viewing" ceremony at the bride's home (Philips, 2004, p. 13). The meeting takes place while the parents and others negotiate the dowry and other matters of mutual interest. The bride- and groom-to-be are "permitted" to move aside and interact for a brief period of time. Meeting for the first time and the context being the ceremonial bride-viewing visit, the prospective partners may not engage in a lengthy interaction. The duration of such meetings could be as brief as ten minutes, and the next time they meet would be at their engagement or wedding. The gender segregation and the societal prohibitions of premarital relationships add to the breadth and intensity of this mutual ignorance (D'Cruz and Bharat, 2001; Jacobson, 1996; Khatri, 1975; Philips, 2004; Singh, 2005). Given this background, marriage, for many Indian couples, is a quick transition from being strangers to becoming spouses.

Although no consensus among researchers exists about what exactly constitutes marital or relationship quality, most researchers agree that marital or relationship quality is associated with couples' health and well-being (Allendorf and Ghimire, 2013; Bradbury et al., 2000; Fincham and Bradbury, 1987; Pimentel, 2000). The discrepant data in the existing literature on arranged marriages in India raised many questions about the health and well-being of couples in those marriages. When those marriages are reportedly plagued by high rates of abuse and intimate partner violence, lack of freedom in the choice of partners, interference of extended families in couples' day-to-day lives, and burdensome practices such as the dowry system and consanguineous marriages, the reports of high levels of marital satisfaction appear to be inconsistent and in need of further examination. The current study was designed to address these concerns and gain deeper insights into the nature of relationship quality in such marriages.

THE PURPOSE STATEMENT

The purpose of this study was to explore the phenomenon of relationship quality in arranged marriages in India. In the context of the changing scenario in the state of marriages across the globe, researchers, particularly in the Western countries, have been identifying features associated with both happy and troubled marriages (Gottman, 1999). Marriages that were found to be healthy, happy, and enduring were often characterized by couples' ability to fulfill each other's important needs, develop intimate and passionate feelings for each other, invest many resources into the relationship, remain committed even in the face of difficulties, create shared goals and values, form and maintain attachment bonds and healthy emotional connection, and engage in healthy reciprocal interactions (Gottman and Gottman, 2008; Hughes, 2007; Rusbult et al., 1998). These characteristics, in short, explicate what accounts for a high level of relationship quality in such marriages. Since these were identified as the essential characteristics for a healthy, happy, and enduring marriage in the context of marriages of choice in the Western countries, it was worth exploring whether the arranged marriages in India were characterized by these qualities. Such an exploration was expected to give a better understanding of the quality of relationship in such marriages.

Based on the above listed characteristics of happy and healthy marriages, the specific constructs chosen for examination in this study were marital satisfaction, quality of alternatives, investments, intimacy, passion, and commitment. Several excellent studies (e.g., Chawla, 2007; Ganguly-Scrase, 2003; Sandhya, 2009; Singh, 2005; Srinivasan and Lee, 2004) have been conducted on arranged marriages in India, but none of them have specifically explored relationship quality in such marriages from the perspective of all these dimensions. Even the studies that looked into some of these constructs were limited in their scope and methods. The current study explored the level of each of these six constructs in the lives of the respondents and examined the association of these constructs with their relationship quality. Individuals who are currently living in arranged marriages in India completed a set of measures assessing different dimensions of marriage. The researcher then contacted a small sample of volunteers from the large sample who completed the questionnaires, and conducted follow-up one-on-one, face-to-face interviews with them.

The researcher used a concurrent triangulation mixed methods design for the current study. Following this methodology, the researcher collected quantitative and qualitative data concurrently, and then compared "the two databases to determine if there was convergence, differences, or some combination" (Creswell, 2009, p. 213). Ideally, both the quantitative and qualitative methods are to be given equal weight in a concurrent triangulation design (Creswell, 2009), and the current study attempted to do that. The quantitative phase consisted of a survey method. The qualitative phase involved one-on-one, face-to-face phenomenological interviews between the researcher and the participants. For the survey, the researcher used multiple instruments and collected data from 287 individuals who are currently living in arranged marriages in India. For the phenomenological interviews, the researcher used an open-ended questionnaire, and fourteen individuals participated in the interviews.

Because arranged marriages in India are a complex phenomenon, a combination of both quantitative and qualitative methods was considered a better approach to study the relationship quality in such marriages. While the quantitative phase gave the researcher numerical data about the participants' level of relationship quality (quantifying the phenomenon), the qualitative phase gave him an opportunity to listen to the participants' thoughts and feelings about the phenomenon (non-quantifiable aspects of the phenomenon). The participants had an opportunity to indicate the level of their relationship quality not only in numbers but also in words. Sometimes the data that emerge from face-to-face, in-depth interviews with participants may be related to the data that is obtained from the quantitative method. However, it is also possible that new data that are totally unrelated to or have little to do with quantitative measures emerge in qualitative interviews. Keeping that in mind, a combination of both methods was chosen to expand the researcher's understanding of the phenomenon of relationship quality.

2

Theoretical Background

THERE WERE FIVE DISTINCT and yet closely related theories that informed the current study on the relationship quality in arranged marriages in India. They are: the investment model (Rusbult et al., 1998), the triangular theory of love (Sternberg, 1986, 1997, 2003), the sound relationship house theory (Gottman and Gottman, 2008), the ecological theory of human development (Bronfenbrenner, 1979), and the attachment theory (Bowlby, 1988, 2005). Each of these theories is briefly described here below.

THE INVESTMENT MODEL

The investment model, developed by Rusbult et al. (1998), suggested that commitment and its three antecedents, satisfaction, quality of alternatives, and investment of resources, determined persistence in marriage and the overall relationship quality. Satisfaction, quality of alternatives, and investment of resources create a psychological inducement for partners to depend on each other. That dependence strengthens their commitment and consequently generates a higher quality of relationship. The basic constructs of the investment model provided a theoretical and conceptual foundation for the current study on arranged marriages in India. Dependence, one of the basic constructs of the investment model, for example, is an all too familiar concept for the people in India. Social interdependence is a defining character of an Indian's life (Jacobson, 1996). Families and communities maintain strong networks of kinship and social ties.

This feature of interdependence is an organizing factor not only for individuals but also for couples in arranged marriages. The question is whether dependence in the Indian context meant the same thing, as it was understood in the investment model. To find that out, it was important to examine whether a high level of marital satisfaction, consideration of the current relationship as the best alternative, and investment of many resources characterized the arranged marriages in India. Couples could be unhappy and yet depend on each other and persist in their marriage due to other reasons such as fear of social isolation and economic instability. According to the investment model, persistence and higher functioning in relationships have to be preceded by a high level of commitment, a high level of satisfaction, poorer alternatives, and large investment size. While high persistence rate in the Indian arranged marriages is already established (Batabyal, 2001), the current study explored whether the investment model was applicable in the Indian context. This theory will be discussed more in detail in chapter 6.

THE TRIANGULAR THEORY OF LOVE

Sternberg (1986, 1997) proposed a different theory to explain relationship quality. According to his triangular theory of love, the three ingredients of successful and loving relationships are intimacy, passion, and decision/commitment. Commitment is a common construct shared by both the investment model and triangular theory of love, but both theories differ about the exact nature of commitment. According to Sternberg, the three components of love interact with each other, and different combinations of these components give rise to different kinds of love. For example, a combination of intimacy and commitment gives rise to companionate love. Similarly, a combination of intimacy and passion gives rise to romantic love. A complete love, which he calls consummate love, is the result of the full combination of all three components of intimacy, passion, and commitment. In such a love, the amount of love in all the three areas of intimacy, passion, and commitment will be large, and there will be a more or less equal balance of the three components (Sternberg, 1986).

In its application to marital relationships, the theory proposes that a loving and affective relationship between partners becomes possible when they possess a large amount of love in the three areas of intimacy, passion, and decision/commitment, and find a more or less equal balance between all of them. In some relationships such as arranged marriages, Sternberg (1986) opined, the three components of love might be highly imbalanced at the beginning of the relationship. Intimacy and passion might be very marginal while decision/commitment might be overemphasized. The current study examined whether the three components of love, intimacy, passion, and decision/commitment, were more or less equally matched in the present-day arranged marriages in India. More details of this theory will be discussed in reference to the conceptual framework of the current study in chapter 6.

THE SOUND RELATIONSHIP HOUSE THEORY

The core ideas of the investment model and triangular theory of love are also related to another theory of marital success that has gained much attention in the recent past, the sound relationship house theory, proposed by John M. Gottman and Julie S. Gottman (2008). Based on several studies of couples across the life course, Gottman and Gottman suggested that couples could be assigned to two broad categories: the "masters of relationships" and the "disasters." The masters of relationships are couples "who remained stable and relatively happy across time" (p. 139), while the disasters are couples "who either broke up or stayed unhappily together" (p. 139). According to the authors, the spousal relationship of the masters is equivalent to a house with seven levels.

The seven levels of the relationship house are: building love maps (knowing one's partner's inner psychological world), sharing fondness and admiration (expressing affection and respect in small everyday moments), turning toward (recognizing the partner's need for emotional connection and turning toward him or her instead of turning away), allowing positive sentiment override (not taking partner's negative or neutral actions personally but approaching them positively), managing conflict (learning to handle perpetual problems and solvable problems appropriately), making life dreams come true (creating an environment to talk about each other's hopes, aspirations, and values freely), and creating shared meaning (creating shared goals and values and establishing certain rituals of connection). The masters of relationships, or stable and happy couples, give adequate attention to these levels of the relationship house, whereas unstable and unhappy couples neglect all or many of these components of the relationship house.

The sound relationship house theory offered a good framework to look at the quality of relationship in arranged marriages in India. The theory suggests that successful marital relationships require partners to consistently promote positive affect and commitment. Persistence in marriage, according to the theory, is not necessarily indicative of stability and satisfaction in marriage. They may not break up but stay married, and yet they could be escalating in their conflicts and negative affect toward each other. When applied to the arranged marriages in India, the theory meant that the low divorce rate and the high persistence in such marriages were not necessarily indicative of healthy and happy relationships. Couples in such marriages could be persisting in their relationship due to other reasons. An examination of constructs such as satisfaction, quality of alternatives, investments, intimacy, passion, and commitment were expected to throw more light on these questions, and the current study looked into them.

THE ECOLOGICAL THEORY OF HUMAN DEVELOPMENT

The ecological systems theory of human development (Bronfenbrenner, 1979) focuses on how social ecology influences the growth and development of an individual. Two major concepts of this theory are the environment and dyadic relationship development. These two concepts were utilized in service of the current study on arranged marriages in India. According to the theory, a person's environment facilitates his or her growth and development. A healthy and supportive environment promotes the development of the person, while a disruptive environment interferes with or inhibits development. Bronfenbrenner, the developer of the theory, grouped the whole environment that supports or interferes with the development of an individual or dyad into four categories: microsystem (the immediate environment, consisting of family members, relatives, friends, peers, neighbors, school, faith community, etc.), mesosystem (the interaction or interconnectedness between the various microsystems, such as home and school), exosystem (the settings that indirectly affect the immediate environment of the developing person), and macrosystem (the overarching patterns of values, ideologies, norms, and culture of the society that influence all other settings of the environment and ultimately affect the person).

The concept of dyadic relationship development pertains to three major phases in the development of a dyadic relationship. First, the dyad begins as an observational dyad, where one member shows significant interest in the life and activities of the other, and the other, in turn, acknowledges that interest being shown. They don't participate or engage in each other's activities at this stage; rather, they stay as observers. In the second phase, they move a little closer to each other by engaging in joint activities. They complement each other in accomplishing a common task. More joint activities will enhance the development of their dyadic relationship. A joint activity also helps to build the three main characteristics of all dyadic relationships—that is, reciprocity, balance of power, and affective relation. In the third phase, they become a primary dyad by growing in their affective feelings for each other and influencing each other's behavior. They will have strong emotional feelings for each other even when they are not together. Their feelings for each other will influence their behavior. Moving into this stage of relationship, according to Bronfenbrenner (1979), is a sign of strong and enduring relationship.

In a marital relationship, the strength and quality of a couple's relationship would depend on their ability to transition from being an observational dyad to a primary dyad. In marriages of choice, one could assume that couples move from being an observational dyad into a primary dyad before they get married. The time of courtship and dating is presumably a time when they grow in their affective feelings for each other and influence each other's behavior. They grow and develop as one unit rather than as two isolated individuals. Marriage then facilitates the continuation and permanence of that bond and relationship.

In arranged marriages, the development of the dyadic relationship is a post-marital task. Since couples come into marriage without knowing much about each other, they first get married and then go through the different stages of the dyadic relationship development. They begin as strangers or as an observational dyad, and then gradually move into the other phases of development. In the arranged marriages in India, moving into the second phase of the dyadic relationship—that is, engaging in joint activities—is presumably an easy task due to the collectivistic nature of the society. Interdependence or reciprocal behaviors are the bedrock of the Indian societal and family systems (Jacobson, 1996). However, it is not clear whether Indian couples are satisfactorily coordinating their activities and engaging in healthy behaviors and interactions. They could be engaging in reciprocal activities out of obligation without having any positive feelings toward each other. If that happens, they would not transition into the phase of a primary dyad, where they would grow in their affective feelings for each other and positively influence each other. Thus, the state of their dyadic relationship would speak to the quality of their marital relationship. The current study looked into these questions.

Bronfenbrenner's ecological theory also provides a framework for taking note of the importance of the ecological factors in the human experience. The collectivistic and culturally embedded lives of Indians point to many ecological factors influencing couples' relationship quality. "Success" in their marital and family life is subject to the fulfillment of their familial, social, and religious duties (Chawla, 2007; Natrajan and Thomas, 2002). Bronfenbrenner's idea regarding the consistency of values across settings influencing the overall development of the person or dyad, a concept that he calls the macrosystem, offers some rationale for the high persistence rate in the Indian arranged marriages. The consistency of community and collectivist values in the culture could be an influencing factor for the high persistence rate in such marriages.

THE ATTACHMENT THEORY

Originally developed by John Bowlby (1988), the attachment theory touches on the impact of attachment experiences on an individual or couple's functioning. Attachment, according to Bowlby, is the proximity or closeness that a child seeks and maintains with the parent or caregiver who is deemed to be better able to cope with a frightening and uncertain world. Bowlby stressed the need for a safe haven and secure caregiving for the formation of strong attachment bonds. Referring to the early childhood experiences, Bowlby suggested that happy, healthy, and positively oriented adolescents and adults are products of strong and stable homes where parents or parent figures provide consistent, safe, and secure caregiving to their children. The attachment bond between the child and the caregiver is solidified not only because the child feels safe and secure but also because the caregiver feels rewarded in meeting those needs of the child (Sayre et al., 2010; Szalavitz and Perry, 2010).

Bowlby also suggested that such patterns of attachment were not confined to childhood alone but rather extended to all age groups and stages of life. Just as a secure and strong attachment bond between the child and the caregiver is essential for the healthy development of a child, a strong attachment bond between adults is necessary for a "well-functioning adulthood" (Sayre et al., 2010, p. 2). A healthy family or relationship, according to Hughes (2004, 2007, 2009) and Sayre et al. (2010), is one in which the members are securely attached to each other. Several other authors (Ainsworth, 1979; Diamond et al., 2007; Hazan and Diamond, 2000; Herring and Kaslow, 2002; Hill et al., 2003; Keiley, 2002; Leon and Jacobvitz, 2003; Mikulincer et al., 2002; Wampler et al., 2003) also have indicated that there is a close association between a sense of attachment security and the quality of relationships in family or adult relationships.

The concepts of safe haven and secure caregiving are akin to Bronfenbrenner's (1979) idea of healthy environment that is necessary for a healthy development. Similarly, the idea of the formation of strong attachment bonds in relationships sounds similar to Bronfenbrenner's idea of the formation of primary dyads, which is the key to successful relationships. The formation of strong attachment bonds in relationships is also similar to the idea of the construction of a sound relationship house in the sound relationship house theory.

Among the different variants of adult relationships, the marital relationship is one area where the theme of attachment gains a special significance. According to Sayre et al. (2010), a strong attachment bond formed by mutual marital caregiving is the hallmark of a well-functioning marital life. The concepts of attachment bonds and positive affective relation are the highlights of emotionally focused couples therapy (EFT), one of the prominent therapy models in the treatment of couples and families. Susan Johnson (2003), one of the developers of the model, summarized the focus of the treatment: "The emotionally focused approach is based on an attachment model of adult intimacy and focuses on restructuring key emotional responses and interactions to create a more secure bond between partners" (p. 366). Because Indian couples have little or very limited knowledge of each other prior to their marriage, it was assumed that it might not be easy for them to form attachment bonds at the beginning of their relationship. However, it was thought that the Indian society being collectivistic in nature, the couple's inevitable need for interdependence might function as a psychological inducer for them to move in that direction. Besides, if the couples had consistent, safe, and secure attachment experiences in their own families of origin, they would naturally be disposed to form stable and happy relationships with their spouses. The data gathered in the current study provided support for these assumptions.

RESEARCH QUESTIONS

The primary research question that directed this study was:

1. What is the relationship quality in arranged marriages in India?

    From this primary question, a number of more specific questions unfolded:

2. What is the level of marital satisfaction in arranged marriages in India, and is there an association between marital satisfaction and relationship quality in such marriages?

3. What is the level of the quality of alternatives in arranged marriages in India, and is there an association between the quality of alternatives and relationship quality in such marriages?

4. What is the level of investment of resources in arranged marriages in India, and is there an association between the investment of resources and relationship quality in such marriages?

5. What is the level of intimacy in arranged marriages in India, and is there an association between intimacy and relationship quality in such marriages?

6. What is the level of passion in arranged marriages in India, and is there an association between passion and relationship quality in such marriages?

7. What is the level of commitment in arranged marriages in India, and is there an association between commitment and relationship quality in such marriages?

8. Is there a difference between men and women in arranged marriages in India in their assessment of satisfaction, quality of alternatives, investments, intimacy, passion, commitment, and the overall relationship quality?

DEFINITION OF TERMS

- *Arranged Marriage:* A marriage that is "fixed or arranged by parents or elders on behalf of and with or without the consent of the boy or the girl involved" (Singh, 2005, p. 143).

- *Relationship Quality:* The quality of marital or spousal relationship in reference to dimensions such as satisfaction, mutual understanding, caring, validation, commitment, intimacy, and positive and affective interaction (Allendorf and Ghimire, 2013; Fletcher et al., 2000; Hendrick, 1988).

- *Marital Satisfaction:* The extent to which marital partners are able to fulfill each other's most important needs and maintain happiness in their marriage (Myers et al., 2005; Rusbult et al., 1998).

- *Perceived Alternatives:* A partner's available alternatives outside of the current marital relationship to fulfill his or her most important needs (Rusbult et al., 1998).

- *Investment Size:* The resources that a partner attaches to the spousal relationship (Rusbult et al., 1998).

- *Intimacy:* Feelings of closeness, connectedness, and affection that a person feels for his or her spouse or marital partner (Heller and Wood, 2000; Moore et al., 2001; Sternberg, 1986).

- *Passion:* "The drives that lead to romance, physical attraction, sexual consummation, and related phenomena in loving relationships" (Sternberg, 1986, p. 1).

- *Commitment:* A partner's sense of allegiance and love toward his or her spouse and the intent to maintain and persist in that love relationship (Rusbult et al., 1998; Sternberg, 1986).

- *Concurrent Triangulation Mixed Methods:* A mixed methods research design in which the researcher collects quantitative and qualitative data concurrently and compares the database to understand a research problem (Creswell, 2009).

PART II

Literature Review

3

Marriages Across the Globe

MARRIAGE CONTINUES TO BE one of the prime institutions in all societies across the globe, except perhaps among the Na people in the Yunnan Province of southwestern China (Coontz, 2005; Musick and Bumpass, 2012; Myers et al., 2005; Sweetman, 2003). The Na people, Coontz (2005) reported, place sibling relationships above all other relationships. This is a community without husbands or wives. In this community of approximately thirty thousand people, brothers and sisters live together, and they jointly raise, educate, and support the children who are born to the sisters through casual romantic encounters. In all other communities and cultures around the world, marriage is one of the major institutions around which people organize their personal and social lives (Broderick, 1992; Coontz, 2005; Mburugu and Adams, 2005; Sheng, 2005; Singh, 2005).

As a socially constructed institution, marriage determines people's rights and obligations with regard to sexuality, gender roles, legitimacy of children, relationships with in-laws, so on and so forth (Broderick, 1992; Coontz, 2005). Rhyne (1981) referred to marriage as "a dramatic act in which two people come together and redefine themselves and the world" (p. 942). Authors such as Bradbury and Karney (2010), Gottman (1999), and Myers et al. (2005) give detailed descriptions about how marriage contributes to the physical and psychological well-being, companionship, greater connection to the larger society, economic stability, and longevity of life for both men and women. There is a wide range of agreement among researchers that men and women are not meant to live alone and that "marriage makes people happier" (Waite and Gallagher, as cited in Musick and Bumpass, 2012, p. 1).

DEFINITIONS AND PRACTICES

Family and marriage scholars (e.g., Azadarmaki, 2005; Coontz, 2005; Modo, 2005; Ziehl, 2005) have come to the conclusion that although marriage is a significant institution in most of the cultures and countries across the globe, societies differ in the way it is defined and contracted. There are also specific rules and stipulations in every society about how people should arrange their marriages and accomplish their tasks (Coontz, 2005). Harvey (2005) and Broderick (1992) noted that in societies where monogamy is the norm (e.g., Canada, United States, and several countries in Europe), marriage is defined as a legal union between a man and a woman involving sexual interaction, common domicile, and procreation of children. The eminent anthropologist, George Peter Murdock (as cited in Coontz, 2005) defined marriage in similar terms: "a universal institution that involves a man and a woman living together, engaging in sexual activity, and cooperating economically" (p. 26).

However, studies have shown that monogamy is not a universal phenomenon. In several African countries (e.g., Kenya, Nigeria, and South Africa), polygyny (a man having multiple wives) is a common phenomenon (Mburugu and Adams, 2005; Modo, 2005; Ziehl, 2005). For example, in Nigeria, each man can marry as many women as he is capable of, provided he is able to care for them and their children (Modo, 2005). Nigerian Muslim men are religiously permitted to have a maximum of four wives, whereas a Nigerian Christian man is expected to have only one wife. If the Christian man had more than one wife before he became a Christian he is permitted to keep his wives. Polygyny has been prevalent among certain sections of the society in India and Iran as well (Azadarmaki, 2005; Chacko, 2003; Singh, 2005). There are also reports of polyandry (a woman having multiple husbands) being practiced in many societies. In parts of Tibet, India, and Nepal, a woman may be married to two or more brothers (Coontz, 2005). Likewise, in Nigeria, among the Rukuba, a wife can take a lover at the time of her first marriage (Coontz, 2005).

There are also several other meanings and practices attached to marriage in communities and cultures around the world. In China and Sudan, there are reported to be what is called ghost or spirit marriages in which a young person is given in marriage to the dead son or daughter of another family, in order to forge closer ties between the two sets of relatives (Coontz, 2005). In many societies (e.g., United States, Germany, Austria, Portugal), marriage between close relatives is discouraged and even prohibited (Amaro, 2005; Klein and Nauck, 2005; Richter and Kytir, 2005; Settles, 2005). However, in countries such as India, Iran, South Africa, and Turkey, consanguineous marriages (marriage between blood relatives) are highly prevalent in many communities (Azadarmaki, 2005; Nauck and Klaus 2005; Singh, 2005; Ziehl, 2005). Cross-cousin marriages and uncle-niece marriages are common in many such communities.

In the Igbo tribe in Nigeria, if an old woman is the only survivor in her family, she might marry a girl (gynaegamy; woman-to-woman marriage) to preserve her family's name (Modo, 2005). The girl could produce children for the old woman by having relations with a male lover. Harvey (2005) stated that with certain countries legalizing same-sex unions over the last few years (e.g., Canada, United States), the concept of marriage has acquired a new meaning. Although in many communities and cultures marriage has been traditionally defined as a union between a man and a woman, these recent instances of the legalization of same-sex unions in some countries point to the possibility of marriage being defined as a union between two persons.

MATE SELECTION AND SEXUAL NORMS

There have been several excellent studies (e.g., Forsberg, 2005; Harvey, 2005; Singh, 2005; Zaidi and Shuraydi, 2002) done on mate selection and sexual norms across countries and cultures around the world. Researchers have found that countries and cultures differ in the way marital partners are chosen. In individualistic cultures (e.g., United States, Canada, and several countries in Europe), where romantic marriages or marriages of choice are the norm, individuals select their prospective marital partners (Applbaum, 1995; De Vaus, 2005; Dumon, 2005; Forsberg, 2005; Harvey, 2005; Madathil and Benshoff, 2008), whereas in collectivistic cultures (e.g., India, Pakistan, China), parents or families are actively involved in the selection of mates for their individual members (Al Naser, 2005; Azadarmaki, 2005; Chen and Yi, 2005; Katz and Lavee, 2005; Lee, 2005; Singh, 2005; Zang, 2008).

Even within marriages of choice and arranged marriages there are variations. For example, in Portugal, although mate selection is mainly dependent on couple's own free initiative, in some families, mothers attentively follow their children's dates and try to influence their partner selection (Amaro, 2005). In the Scandinavian countries of Denmark, Norway, and Sweden, the tradition of dating does not exist as a concept (Trost and Levin, 2005). In those countries, if couples are engaged, it means they have decided to marry. In Israel, while parents and families arrange marriages in the ultraorthodox Jewish community, the Arabs follow a system of semi-arranged marriages (Katz and Lavee, 2005). Among Arabs, parents have some say in mate selection, but young men and women choose their own marital partners. Since free encounters between unmarried men and women in the village are not accepted, they meet outside the village or away from their home.

In reference to mate selection, several authors (e.g., Azadarmaki, 2005; Katz and Lavee, 2005; Richter and Kytir, 2005) have noted that societies differ in the way people perceive sexual and premarital relationships. While widespread acceptance of premarital sex and relationships in certain societies exists, sexual contact outside of marriage is prohibited and even punishable in others. In countries such as Austria, Australia, and Finland, premarital sex is widely accepted (Richter and Kytir, 2005; De Vaus, 2005; Forsberg; 2005). In Austria, most adolescents have sexual intercourse between ages sixteen and nineteen (Richter and Kytir, 2005). On the other hand, in counties such as India, Iran, and Kuwait, premarital sex is prohibited or discouraged (Singh, 2005; Azadarmaki, 2005; Al Naser, 2005). In Kuwait, an Islamic country, where the Islamic law or Sharia guides marriage laws and norms, sexual contact outside of marriage is a punishable offense (Al Naser, 2005). Among the ultraorthodox Jews in Israel, the community does not permit dating, and hence premarital sex or sexual contacts before marriage is strictly prohibited (Katz and Lavee, 2005).

TASKS AND TRANSACTIONS

Coontz (2005) gives a detailed description of what marriages did and continue to do for individual and societies across the world. She opined that for thousands of years, marriage was about "property and politics" (p. 9). It "converted strangers into relatives and extended cooperative relations beyond the immediate family or small band" (p. 6). It helped people to organize their sexual behavior, living arrangements, and child rearing. It was a way to consolidate wealth, pool resources, and forge political and military alliances. Peace treaties were concluded by strategically marrying off their sons and daughters. The dowry, bride-wealth, or tribute exchanged through marriage was a large investment that couples and their parents made for their future. Marriage was the primary "source of social security, medical care, and unemployment insurance" (p. 7). Because marriage was an important economic and political contract, many others such as relatives, neighbors, judges, priests, and government officials were involved in the matchmaking process and marital arrangements.

As an economic transaction, bridewealth or dowry, by which the contracting parties negotiated and exchanged money or goods, was and still continues to be an important part of marriages in many cultures. However, studies have shown that societies differ in the way these transactions take place. For example, in Nigeria, bridewealth refers to the transfer of assets from the boy's family to the girl's family (Modo, 2005). In South Africa, particularly among the black communities, bridewealth has both an economic and symbolic meaning (Ziehl, 2005). It is considered more as "childwealth" in the sense that the assets transferred are seen as compensation that the boy's family is paying to the girl's family for the loss of control over her reproductive capacity (Ziehl, 2005). In other words, since children born through marriage will be an "asset" to the groom's family rather than to the bride's family, the bridewealth is the groom's way of compensating the bride's family for their loss. In India, dowry is the most prevalent practice (Singh, 2005). Most marriage transactions in India involve the bride's family paying dowry in terms of cash or goods or both to the groom's family.

With regard to the sharing of tasks, for hundreds and perhaps thousands of years, men, women, and children shared the tasks of breadwinning in the family (Coontz, 2005). The "tradition" of women staying home as full-time homemakers and men working outside as main earners and breadwinners for the family, according to Coontz (2005), is only a recent development that began in the late eighteenth century, particularly in Western Europe and North America. In some societies, even when women had full employment outside, they still had to be perfect housewives, do all the household jobs, and care for their children (Toth and Somlai, 2005).

RADICAL SHIFTS IN FOCUS

Coontz (2005), who did extensive research on the history of marriage, noted that there have been many radical shifts in the focus of marriage from time to time. According to her, for most of human history, the primary focus of marriage was not the fulfillment of individual needs and desires. People fell in love, but marriage was not basically about love. It was a combination of many things such as getting good in-laws, increasing the family's work force by finding a lifetime companion, and raising children. However, toward the end of the eighteenth century there was a shift in the focus of marriage in some societies. People in several countries in Europe and North America began to emphasize the new idea of love being the central focus of marriage. They also began to emphasize the freedom for young people to choose their marital partners on the basis of love and personal relationship and challenged the right of families or outsiders to intrude upon their lives and mate selection. These marriages came to be known as romantic marriages or marriages of choice. Today, this kind of marriage, which respects individual freedom in mate selection and expects love as the focal point of marriage, is the norm in many cultures and communities around the world, particularly in Europe, North America, and South America (Broderick, 1992; De Vaus, 2005; Harvey, 2005; Toth and Somlai, 2005).

4

The Institution of Marriage in India

As CHEKKI (1988) NOTED, there has been a "proliferation of studies" (p. 173) on India, Indian family systems, and Indian marriages. While Guha (2007) researched the history of India, Singh (2005) studied the contemporary Indian family. Researchers such as Chacko (2003), Chawla (2006, 2007), Chekki (1996), Medora (2007), Philips (2004), and Sandhya (2009) added to the knowledge base on Indian marriages, particularly arranged marriages. The following sections look into some of these studies and give an overview of Indian family system and the institution of marriage.

FAMILY SYSTEM IN INDIA

Although it is difficult to present a unified picture of the Indian family system due to the unfathomable diversity and complexity of the society, Indian families, by and large, are patriarchal, hierarchical, and caste-and class-ridden (Bose and South, 2003; Chekki, 1988; Jacobson, 1996; Medora, 2007; Singh, 2005). The authority within the family is chiefly in the hands of the senior male member of the family. Family members render respect, loyalty, submissiveness, and deference to the authority figure.

In this patriarchal and hierarchical system, women often suffered the most. Although deference to authority is demanded in other relationships in the family as well, such as children to their parents, wives to her husbands, and younger brothers to their older brothers, women often found themselves placed in a subservient position (Bose and South, 2003; Chekki, 1988). Women were expected to be dutiful and obedient to men. There was a time when at meals, women customarily served men first, and ate only after they finished. A wife customarily followed behind her husband when the two walked together. She avoided uttering his name or addressing him by his name lest it be taken as disrespectful. There are contradictory messages with regard to the behaviors toward women. Chekki (1996) cited some of such contradictory texts in *Manusmrithi*, one of the ancient law books in Hinduism. In this book, everyone is called upon to show utmost respect to women, but at the same time the book would say that women do not deserve to be free.

Vanita (2003) elaborated on this religious stipulation and suggested that in Indian society, a woman is to be subordinate to men by being under the protection of her father in youth, husband in adulthood, and son in old age. In her research on Indian families, Khalakdina (2008) also found this contradiction between how women are portrayed in religious beliefs and how they are treated in real life situations. In religious beliefs, the female figure is deified (*devi*; Sanskrit word for goddess), while in real life situations she is discounted. With the rise in education and other societal changes, there have been considerable changes in people's perception of women's role in Indian families (Singh, 2005).

In some places, women have taken the lead in initiating changes in the rigid patriarchal mind-set. One of the participants in Chawla's (2006) ethnographic study on Indian Hindu women in arranged marriages described how she was branded a "radical" when she took a strong stand against the discriminatory patriarchal systems in India. The participant, Radhika, who was a medical doctor by profession, broke her prearranged engagement with her fiancé because he questioned her strong views of the patriarchal structure of the medical profession. Chawla noted that although calls for such "radical" changes in the social systems are reported every now and then, patterns of behavior that echo the mind-set of the patriarchal and hierarchical family system are still prevalent in many parts of India.

India is a caste- and class-ridden society, making the families and communities limit their interactions and social connections to their own particular castes and classes (Medora, 2007; Natrajan, 2005; Vaid and Heath, 2010). There are hundreds of distinct castes, sub-castes, and communities dispersed over the whole country (Jacobson, 1996). Caste is ascribed at birth and a person born into a particular caste cannot alter it. In the traditional caste system, which many Hindus believed was divinely ordained, people were classified into four major castes: *Brahmins, Kshatriyas,*

Vaishyas, and *Shudras* (Medora, 2007). When it was rigidly prevalent and practiced, the caste affiliations dictated the behavior and life chances of individuals in the society. The members of the high caste, *Brahmins*, for example, enjoyed economic prosperity while the low caste people such as *Shudras* were at a position of poverty and social disadvantage.

Sanctioned by the community, the caste system thus institutionalized inequality and discrimination in the society (Medora, 2007). The practice of caste system is unconstitutional in India today. And with the societal changes in the twentieth century, especially with the economic liberalization that began in the 1990s, virtually all castes began to find their members in different class positions such as agricultural laborers, daily-wage workers, rich landlords, industrial laborers, and capitalist farmers and businessmen (Joshi, 2010; Natrajan, 2005). However, studies have shown that the caste system is still determining the behavior of people in many communities and regions (Medora, 2007; Singh, 2005).

With regard to the living arrangements of families, studies show that multiple family patterns have coexisted for many centuries in India (D'Cruz and Bharat, 2001; Singh, 2005). There have been joint families, nuclear families, and single-parent families coexisting in the Indian society (D'Cruz and Bharat, 2001; Medora, 2007). It is not uncommon to see parents or parents-in-law living with a couple or clusters of relatives living close to each other in the same neighborhood or locality (Jacobson, 1996). Living in extended households or in proximity to one's kith and kin helps them to be easily accessible and available to each other to meet their kinship obligations. Such living arrangements have advantages such as supporting the aged, the ill, the widowed, and the disabled, sharing resources and expenditures, and sharing the responsibilities such as childrearing (Ram and Wong, 1994).

Although most families are organized on patrilineal (tracing descent and inheritance in the male line) norms, family systems based on matrilineal (tracing the descent and inheritance in the female line) norms also are prevalent in some regions of the country (Chacko, 2003; Khalakdina, 2008). The high caste Nayars of Kerala and the tribal groups of Khasis, Garos, and Pnars in the northeastern states of India are reported to be matrilineal (Philips, 2004).

MARRIAGES IN INDIA

Most Indians believe in the inevitability of marriage (Bose and South, 2003; Hoelter et al., 2004; Singh, 2005). Scholars such as Bose and South (2003), Chawla (2007), and Chekki (1996) have extensively researched Indian marriages, especially Hindu marriages. They found that Hindu religious texts such as *Vedas*, *Smrithis*, and *Upanishads* considered marriage as a duty and sacrament that was required of all human beings. For a Hindu, there are four main goals in life (Chawla, 2007): *kaama* (emotional, sexual, and aesthetic satisfaction), *artha* (material satisfaction), *dharma* (moral satisfaction/righteousness), and *moksha* (spiritual satisfaction/liberation). An ideal Hindu accomplishes these four goals through the four stages of his or her life—that is, *brahmacharya* (discipline and education), *grahastha* (life of the householder and active worker), *vanaprastha* (retreat for the loosening of material and social bonds), and *sanyasa* (life of meditation in solitude) (Chawla, 2007; Chekki, 1996). The second stage, *grahastha*, is the stage of marital life, and it is part of one's responsibility to the community and society. It is essential for the continuation of the family line and smooth transfer of inheritance. In this regard, individual interests are secondary to the interests of the family and community (Chekki, 1996).

Variants of Marriages

Studies (e.g., Philips, 2004; Singh, 2005) show no single system of marriage for the whole of India. Just as the society is immensely complex and diverse, Indian marriages portray a large diversity in their forms and practices. While for some marriage is a way to cast their net wider, creating new alliances, for others it is a way to keep their family ties and kinship intact. Thus, there are both endogamous (marrying within one's own group, caste, or clan) and exogamous (prohibition of marrying within one's own group) marriages prevalent in India (Singh, 2005).

In some communities, the stipulations of endogamy are vehemently enforced. For example, the Knanaya Christian community in Kerala is endogamous to the extent that marriage outside the community invites excommunication of the person from their church (Philips, 2004). Similarly, the Syro-Malabar Catholics in Kerala who claim to be the descendants of the high caste Brahmin and Nayar converts of St. Thomas, the Apostle (one of the disciples of Jesus), are endogamous and hypergamous (marrying into an equal or more prestigious social group or caste). In that community, a marriage with Latin Catholics (Paraya Christians, Pulaya Christians, Nadar Christians), who are generally new converts from lower castes, is often frowned upon and discouraged (Philips, 2004). The majority of Hindu marriages are endogamous in reference to caste. Marrying outside one's caste is discouraged and even considered a disgrace to the family. Although monogamy is the most preferred practice in India, polygyny (a man with multiple wives) and polyandry (a set of men/brothers having a common wife) also exist in some regions of the country (Bose and South, 2003; Caldwell et al., 1983, 1984; Chekki, 1988; Singh, 2005).

Consanguineous marriages (marriage between close kinsmen/blood relatives) are prevalent in many parts of India, particularly in the southern states (Chekki, 1988; Philips, 2004; Singh, 2005). Among these, the most common ones are cross-cousin marriages and uncle-niece marriages. When a girl marries her cousin (her father's sister's son or her mother's brother's son) her aunt becomes her mother-in-law or her uncle becomes her father-in-law. Similarly, when a girl marries her uncle (e.g., mother's brother) her maternal grandmother becomes her mother-in-law and maternal grandfather becomes her father-in-law.

Display of Collectivism

Marriages in India are not just between two individuals but also between two families, two communities, and sometimes even two cultures (Hoelter et al., 2004; Madathil and Benshoff, 2008; Medora, 2007). A wedding in India is an occasion when the collectivistic identity of the Indian society is at its best display (Jacobson, 1996). There is a celebrated meeting of traditional values, kinship bond, social and familial obligations, impassioned sentiments, and an envious display of economic status and resources (Jacobson, 1996).

ARRANGED MARRIAGES IN INDIA

Most marriages in India are arranged marriages. This form of marriage in India has been a fascinating topic for many family and marital studies (e.g., Bose and South, 2003; Chawla, 2006, 2007; Chekki, 1988, 1996; Hoelter et al., 2004; Philips, 2004; Singh, 2005). These and several other scholars have shown that as per the practice in India, parents or elders in the family take the lead in selecting the marital partners and contracting marital alliances for their children. Finding the perfect match for one's son or daughter is a daunting task for parents. They avail various methods to find a good match for their child. Classified matrimonial advertisements in newspapers, marriage bureaus, marriage brokers, and proposals brought by relatives and friends are the different means families use to find potential brides and grooms for their children (Chawla, 2007; Chekki, 1988; Jacobson, 1996). For many Hindus, matching the horoscopes (charts relating to one's birth under certain astrological calculations) of the boy and girl is an important factor in making the mate selection (Chawla, 2006, 2007; Fuller and Narasimhan, 2008; Netting, 2010).

Measure of Participation

The measure of participation in choosing one's life partner varies between groups and communities (Singh, 2005). In most of the arranged marriages in India, prospective brides and grooms have very limited knowledge of each other prior to their marriage (Philips, 2004). They meet only a few times before marriage, and their meeting takes place in the presence of their family. They might see each other's photographs, but if they are not from the same village or neighborhood, the first time they would meet is usually when their parents and other family members meet to negotiate the marriage alliance.

In the state of Kerala, for example, there is a ceremonial "bride-viewing" (*pennu kaanal* in Malayalam, the language of the state) visit to the girl's home by the groom and his immediate family (Philips, 2004). During such ceremonial visits, the bride-to-be is expected to appear or present herself before the groom-to-be and his family, serving them tea or refreshments. In presenting herself she has to have a humble and modest demeanor, knowing that the prospective groom could snub or refuse her. During the bride-viewing visit, the bride and the groom could move aside to meet and interact for a short period of time. Some might meet a couple of times more for such brief periods, but in most cases, the next time they would meet is at their engagement or wedding. If parents and families arrive at a mutually satisfying negotiated decision, boys and girls consent to their decisions and seldom oppose the alliance. Thus, two strangers agree to become spouses through family mediation, and they count on their families to take the alliance forward. The gender segregation and the societal prohibitions of premarital relationships add to the breadth and intensity of couples' lack of knowledge of each other (D'Cruz and Bharat, 2001; Jacobson, 1996; Philips, 2004).

Determinants of Mate Selection

The major determinants for finalizing a marital alliance are the similarity of both families in their social and economic status, caste, religion, and family traditions, the physical complexion and attractiveness of the bride and groom, the behavior of the members of the family, particularly of women, geographical distance between families, dowry, match of horoscopes, and the educational qualifications of the prospective bride and groom (Chawla, 2006, 2007; Fuller and Narasimhan, 2008; Gopalakrishnan and Babacan, 2007; Netting, 2010; Philips, 2004; Yelsma and Athappilly, 1988). Yelsma and Athappilly noted that only if five or more of these requirements were explicitly present, the families would even consider discussing a prospective marriage alliance. All these factors are considered important to consider because parents are not just choosing a wife for their son or husband for their daughter but rather a daughter-in-law or son-in-law who would form the next male or female generation in the family (Caldwell et al., 1983).

Sexual Norms and Expectations

Morality relating to sex is a great value in the Indian society (Batabyal, 2001; Medora, 2007). Sex and sexuality are not topics that are freely talked about in Indian homes. It is a taboo to bring up such matters in family conversations (Medora, 2007). Premarital relationships of any kind have been highly discouraged (D'Cruz and Bharat, 2001; Medora, 2007; Singh, 2005). Even frequent social interactions between boys and girls are looked at with suspicion (Batabyal, 2001). In the past, prenuptial chastity was demanded of both males and females, but gradually it was more expected of women than men. Parents considered it a great blessing to give their virgin daughter in marriage (*kanyadaan*, gift of virgin bride in Sanskrit; Philips, 2004).

By and large, the Indian family system and the institution of marriage in India are as complex and diversified as the country itself.

5

Current Trends and Relationship Quality in Marriages

RESEARCH ON MARRIAGES CONTINUES to grow. As the institution of marriage continues to evolve and acquire new meanings and significance in different times and societies, researchers look into its history, definitions, and practices. Studies have shown that individualistic and collectivistic cultures differ in the way they define and conduct marriages. Although arranged marriages and marriages of choice are not strictly identified with any one culture or country, each of them finds prominence in some societies over others. Arranged marriages, for example, find prominence in India and several of the Asian countries, while marriages of choice are the most common form of marriage in the United States and most of the Western countries. In both these forms of marriage, the researchers have found that there are both positive and negative trends present. The following sections will discuss in some detail these trends in both these forms of marriage.

MARRIAGES OF CHOICE

There is both good news and bad news about the current state of affairs in marriages of choice. The good news is that marriages of choice are neither doomed nor have people lost faith in the role marriages play in bringing health and happiness to individuals and families (Coontz, 2005). The bad news is that there is a rise in the breakdown of such marriages, and there is the consequent disruption in the lives of individuals and families (Coontz, 2005; Gottman, 1999; Hall, 2012; Musick and Bumpass, 2012).

Coontz (2005), in her research on the history of marriage, found that the "institution of marriage has always been in a flux," and she suggested that there is no reason to assume that there had been a "golden age of marriage in the past" (p. 1). However, she also noted that the current happenings in marriages across the globe, particularly in the Western world, are without any "historical precedent" (p. 2). Whether they call it a crisis or a new phase in the history of marriage, marital and family researchers (e.g., Coontz, 2005; Gottman, 1999) agree that there is a great deal of volatility and dramatic changes taking place in the functions, meanings, and arrangement of marriages. Adams and Trost (2005) summarized this in the following words: "The world in which families exist today is a world of economic *globalization*. It is a world of religious, racial, and economic *violence*. It is a world of the internet and CNN, of mass communication, and—as Kerry Daly and Anna Dienhart remind us—of accelerated *time demands*" (p. 603).

Positive Trends

The likelihood of the negative trends in the institution of marriage today diminishing people's desire for marriage cannot be minimized. However, several studies (Bradbury and Karney, 2010; Gottman, 1999; Hall, 2012; Musick and Bumpass, 2012; Myers et al., 2005) indicate that the ideal of marriage is still important and appealing for the general population in Europe, North America, or other places where marriage of choice is the norm. The vast majority of people still choose to marry as opposed to staying single or living in other relationship arrangements (De Vaus, 2005). For example, Harvey (2005) reported that although cohabitation is prevalent in Canada, over 90 percent of Canadians eventually marry. The divorce rate is not alarming in all the industrialized countries either. Amaro (2005) reported that in 2001, divorce rate in Portugal was only 1.9 percent.

There have been also several studies (e.g., Coontz, 2005; Gottman and Gottman, 2008; Rusbult et al., 1998; Sternberg, 1986) done to assess the quality of relationship in romantic marriages or marriages of choice. The results that emerged from those studies indicate that in spite of all the volatility and troubles, many of those marriages are happy, healthy, and stable. In a study of eighty-seven heterosexual couples belonging to three types of relationship status—that is, dating, living together, and married—Moore et al. (2001) found that married couples and couples in longer duration of relationships experienced higher levels of intimacy and relationship satisfaction than other couples. Coontz, in her research on marriage, found that today married people in North America and Western Europe are generally happier, healthier, and better protected against economic setbacks and psychological distress than people in other relationship arrangements. She added that couples work hard to enrich their marital relationship and take it to higher levels of intimacy and satisfaction.

In Israel, Katz and Lavee (2005) observed, people were generally satisfied with their marital quality. They cited a study done by Shaked who found high marital satisfaction among Jewish men and women in Israel. The participants consisted of 1,504 men and women, and the results showed that 74 percent of men and 61 percent of women were very satisfied with their marital relationship. In Australia, De Vaus (2005) found marriages more stable than cohabiting relationships. In Austria, Canada, and the United States, studies have shown that married couples experience high marital satisfaction, mutual love, and intimacy at the beginning of their marriage and at the empty-nest stage (Harvey, 2005; Richter and Kytir, 2005; Settles, 2005). These authors found that in these countries, there is a downturn in marital satisfaction between the times the first child is born and the last child leaves home, but otherwise married couples maintain a high level of intimacy and satisfaction.

Research assessing the difference between marriages of choice and arranged marriages in reference to marital satisfaction has been done. For example, in China, two studies, one by Xiaohe and Whyte (1990) and the other by Jin and Xu (as cited by Bradbury and Karney, 2010), were conducted to compare marital satisfaction in love marriages and arranged marriages. The results showed that people in love marriages (marriage of choice) were more satisfied than those in arranged marriages. In the first study, Xiaohe and Whyte surveyed 586 Chinese women, and the results showed that women having a choice in who they married were reliably more satisfied in their relationship than those whose partners were chosen by the family. In the second study, Jin and Xu interviewed more than 10,000 Chinese couples, and the results showed that love marriages were more satisfying than arranged marriages.

By and large, these studies demonstrate that for many couples in marriages of choice today, their relationship has become more joyful, loving, and satisfying than ever before. Researchers have identified several factors that contribute to the formation of such joyful, loving, and satisfying relationships. In their research on marital relationships in Israel, Katz and Lavee (2005) found that marital satisfaction is an outcome of a sense of bonding, caring, feeling of unity and companionship, mutual understanding, respect, trust, satisfactory sexual relationship, communication, and compatibility (similar mentality, worldview, character, and mutual leisure and social interests). Mirja Tolkki-Nikkonen (as cited in Forsberg, 2005), in a study on Finnish couples, found that couples' ability to accept differences and changes in each other, ability to please each other, commitment, intimacy, valuing of the self, talking, resolving conflicts, and receiving a response to one's expectations are some of the factors that help the formation of loving and long-lasting marital relationships. If social, familial, and financial concerns took precedence over everything else in marriages in the past, factors such as love, intimacy, and satisfaction determine the quality of marriages in many societies today (White et al., 1986).

Negative Trends

One of the negative trends seen prominently in marriages of choice today is the alarming rate of divorce (Gottman, 1999). According to a report that Gottman presented on the disturbing trends in the state of marriages in the United States, the chances of first marriages ending in divorce ranged between 50 percent and 67 percent, and the breakup of second marriages remained on the same level or 10 percent higher. In Austria, the divorce rate was reported to be 46 percent or more (Richter and Kytir, 2005). In Belgium, the figures were more or less the same, 45.1 percent (Dumon, 2005).

Even among those who remain married, many couples live in highly conflicted and emotionally distressing relationships. The crisis has put families and children at the risk of reaping negative consequences and psychological distress (Gottman, 1999). For couples, Gottman observed, some of the negative consequences that arise from the dissolution of their marriage are increased risk of psychopathology, increased rates of automobile accidents, increased incidence of physical illness, suicide, violence, and homicide, and decreased longevity. For children, besides the psychological distress, divorces and separation lead to a life in single-parent families and step- and blended families (De Vaus, 2005). Gottman observed that the changed scenario has raised the ante for marital researchers and therapists. While the former look into the factors that lead to the dysfunction and dissolution of marriages, the latter are busy trying to address and fix the problems faced by couples and families.

Another negative trend is the deinstitutionalization of marriages and the rise in marriage-like relationships and living arrangements (Coontz, 2005; Hall, 2012). The functions and meanings of marriage have become more pluralistic and diverse in many countries, especially in the Western countries (Hall, 2012). De Vaus (2005) observed that many people do not perceive marriage as a necessary component of being a family. Sex, living together, and childbearing, which were once considered functions associated with a marital relationship, take place prior to or outside of marriage in many countries today (Jelin, 2005; Musick and Bumpass, 2012; Toth and Somlai, 2005). According to Cherlin (as cited in Hall, 2012), in the past, people in the United States looked at marriage as a social obligation and organization, but today, for many, it has become more about individual prestige and achievement. Hall, in his study, found that some individuals avoid or have conflicting thoughts about marriage because they perceive it as an institution that reduces their autonomy and forces them to enter into a permanent commitment for which they may not be ready. Many of them like to cohabit with their partner but do not intend to formalize those relationships into a permanent contract or commitment. Thus, in countries such as Australia, Austria, and Czech Republic, there has been a steady decline in the number of people getting married and a rapid increase in cohabitation (De Vaus, 2005; Richter and Kytir, 2005; Mozny and Katrnak, 2005).

In countries such as Germany, Denmark, Norway, and Sweden, "Living apart together (LAT)" is becoming a new alternative to marriage and cohabitation (Klein and Nauck, 2005; Trost and Levin, 2005). Michel Berkiel (as cited in Trost and Levin, 2005), a Dutch journalist, first identified this relationship type in the Netherlands, and coined the term "*LAT relatie*" (p. 357). According to this arrangement, two persons form a couple, living under marriage-like conditions, but they do not share the same home. They live separately and yet define themselves as a steady couple. Thus, the perceptions of marriage vary from seeing it as a permanent commitment of unwavering fidelity to one's partner to considering it as a temporary mutual arrangement that can be broken or changed if either or both parties feel dissatisfied in their personal gratification (see Hall, 2012, and Musick and Bumpass, 2012, for more details on the changed scenario with regard to the functions and meanings of marriage in the Western countries). According to Coontz (2005), the increase in multiple forms of marriage-like relationships have led to either low birthrates (e.g., Germany, Japan) or birth of a large number of children out of wedlock (e.g., United States).

ARRANGED MARRIAGES IN INDIA

As with marriages of choice, the arranged marriages in India also have both good news and bad news. The good news is that those marriages persist and the divorce rate is very low. The bad news is that there are reports of high rates of violence, abuse, and lack of freedom in such marriages.

Positive Trends

The arranged marriages in India are reported to be stable and long lasting (Batabyal, 2001; Singh, 2005). Dissolution of marriages is uncommon and infrequent across the nation except perhaps in some metropolitan cities (Bose and South, 2003; Singh, 2005). Most of the studies pertaining to arranged marriages in India indicate some consistent results with regard to marital satisfaction. For example, Yelsma and Athappilly (1988) compared the levels of marital satisfaction between Indian couples who had an arranged marriage, Indian couples who had a love marriage, and American couples who had a companionate marriage (marriage of choice). The results showed that Indian couples in arranged marriages had a higher level of marital satisfaction than the other two groups.

Likewise, Madathil and Benshoff (2008) conducted a study comparing the levels of marital satisfaction between Indian couples in arranged marriages living in India, Indian couples in arranged marriages living in the US, and American couples in marriages of choice. They found that overall, Indian couples in arranged marriages living in the US were significantly more satisfied with their marriages than the other two groups. In a study of ninety-one Hindu married couples (182 participants) in India, Sandhya (2009) assessed marital happiness, intimacy, good times, and conflict. On a seven-point scale, the mean score on the overall marital happiness was 5.4 ($SD = 1.5$), and 62 percent of the couples reported that they were either very happy or perfectly happy. Another 32 percent reported that they were happy sometimes.

The study conducted by Myers et al. (2005) did not show any significant difference between arranged marriages and marriages of choice with regard to marital satisfaction. Myers and her colleagues examined the relationship between marital satisfaction and holistic wellness in couples living in the United States in marriages of choice and couples living in India in arranged marriages. The data from forty-five individuals in arranged marriages living in India was compared with existing data on married individuals in the US who had marriage of choice. The study found no difference in marital satisfaction between these two groups and that couples in arranged marriages could be as happy and satisfied as couples that had marriages of choice. Likewise, Chawla (2007) cited a study done by Dhyani and Kumar in India in 1992, which investigated the association between type of marriage, marital duration, sexual satisfaction, and adjustment. The participants consisted of 240 Indian married women, and the results indicated that there was no significant relationship between the type of marriage and marital duration with marital adjustment.

Negative Trends

The results of most of the studies discussed above show that arranged marriages in India have a better or equal level of satisfaction in comparison with love marriages or marriages of choice. These findings, of course, do not match with the reports of studies done in China as cited above. In those studies done in China, marriages of choice had higher satisfaction than arranged marriages. The difference could be attributed to cultural differences. However, some of the negative trends present in the Indian arranged marriage would contest such claims. As discussed before, there is solid data to show that the rate of abuses and violence in such marriages in India is enormously high. The reports of cruelty and torture to which men and their families subject their wives do not speak well of those marriages.

Concerning the presence of violence in marriages in India, Chacko (2003) and Singh (2005) stated that the recipients of most of the incidents of violence and abuse are women, and the perpetrators of those crimes are men. For example, in a study conducted in five districts of the state of Uttar Pradesh, 30 percent of men acknowledged that they had physically abused their wives (Singh, 2005). Looking into a community-based study on violence against women, Chacko found that 69 percent of the women sampled in a city in the state of Kerala reported being subjected to some form of violence. According to Singh's report, women "have been victims of humiliation and torture for as long as we have written records of Indian society" (p. 152). Wife-battering, forced incest, coercion, and other kinds of humiliations and abuses mark the life of many women in Indian families (Singh, 2005).

One of the leading causes cited for abuses and violence in Indian arranged marriages is the dowry system (Chaco, 2003; Chawla, 2007; Jacobson, 1996; Philips, 2004; Singh, 2005). Srinivasan and Lee (2004) suggested that the modern-day dowry system had its basis in the age-old practices of *kanyadhan* (gift of virgin bride), *varadhakshina* (gifts given by the bride's father to the groom), and *stridhan* (gifts given by the relatives and friends to the bride). But in contemporary India, dowry has attained a different meaning. Dowry is now considered the right of the groom and his family to demand exorbitant amounts of cash and goods from the bride's family. Although it is called *sthreedhanam*, or gifts given to the bride, Chacko noted that the dowry appropriated by the husband or his family is often used not for her empowerment but rather to "pay off loans, start a new business, or even help pay the dowries of unmarried women in the groom's immediate family" (p. 56).

Failure to meet dowry demands would culminate in the harassment, torture, and even murder of the bride (Singh, 2005). Even when there are such threats, many parents are reluctant to allow their daughters to return home for fear of having to pay a second dowry. Singh (2005) and Shukla (2009) noted that there were many cases of dowry-related abuses and violence that were unreported or underreported. As mentioned previously, two out of every five married women in India reported being hit, kicked, beaten, or slapped by their husbands. Chacko (2003) noted that since domestic violence is considered a personal and private matter, such abuses are often hidden from the public view.

Another negative trend that characterizes the arranged marriages in India is the patriarchal system in which the society favors men over women. An example of male domination and favoritism toward men is the subject of divorce. According to Medora (2007), the society looks more favorably upon men than women in matters concerning divorce. Medora noted that seeking and receiving a divorce is harder for women than men because women are socially and economically dependent on their husbands and their family members. Additionally, Medora stated that even if their husbands initiate the divorce, women and their families are often blamed for the divorce, and they are negatively characterized. Due to all these negative repercussions connected with divorce, many women, Medora noted, "stay within the confines of a tyrannical family as a silent sufferer rather than break away" (p. 185).

Another negative characteristic of arranged marriages in India that is closely associated with the patriarchal structure of the society is the expectation of strict adherence to gender roles and responsibilities, which again favors men over women. Non-adherence to gender roles and responsibilities could result in abuses and disciplinary actions (Singh, 2005). In India, there is a very strong preference for sons, and women are conditioned to accept the secondary position in families (Bose and South, 2003; D'Cruz and Bharat, 2001; Singh, 2005). Sons are preferred to daughters because of the patrilineal society that looks up to the son to continue the family line, contribute to the family income, take care of the parents in their old age, and perform the last rites for their parents (Bose and South, 2003). Daughters, in contrast, incur large expenses for families because of the dowries that are to be paid upon their marriages, and after marriage they transfer their allegiance to their husband's families (Bose and South, 2003; Singh, 2005).

Much of the reported violence against women is due to the non-adherence to gender roles, some of which could be as simple as not cooking on time (Singh, 2005). A woman is expected to hold many roles together. She has to be a mother, efficient housekeeper, and obedient and submissive wife and daughter-in-law. If she fails in one of these roles, her husband or in-laws take her to task. However, Singh observed that surprisingly, the majority of Indian women accept the use of force to discipline them. In his study, Singh learned that three out of five women believed that wife beating was justified, particularly when they neglected the house or child. They accept the right of husbands to use force to discipline them, especially when the wife violates traditional gender norms. Singh also added that women might be accepting such abuses since they feel powerless in the patriarchal society.

Medora (2007) noted that certain beliefs such as those in the law of *karma* (consequence of one's actions), *punarjanma* (reincarnation), and astrology could be another reason for the prevalence of unhealthy behaviors in Indian marriages. The belief in *karma*, for example, makes people believe that they "should be passive and accepting of difficulties in life in order to be rewarded in the next life" (Medora, 2007, p. 179). Such beliefs, Medora noted, encourage passivity and fatalistic attitudes, and consequently discourage any change in the unhealthy system.

Added to all of these negative trends, there is also the tremendous societal pressure put on couples to remain in marriage even if their relationships are toxic and abusive. Since most Indians view marriage and persistence in marriage as sacred duties, staying married even in adverse circumstances is considered a noble act. The society does not treat kindly those who disavow such cultural and religious expectations. If they leave their marriages and seek divorce, they are often subjected to shame and stigma. Studies (Dupree et al., 2013; Medora, 2007) have indicated that the low divorce rate in India could be because of these cultural, religious, and social stigmas associated with divorce.

6

The Conceptual Framework
of the Current Study

THERE IS NO PRETENSE that the review of literature on marriages across the globe and arranged marriages in India gives a comprehensive and exhaustive idea of marriages and marital practices in all cultures and communities around the world. However, the scholarly studies reviewed show that although marriage is one of the most significant institutions in almost every society across the globe, cultures and communities still differ in the way it is defined, conducted, and contracted. The review distinguishes India from several of the individualistic cultures with regard to marital and family life. In the individualistic cultures, especially in the Western countries, one view holds that individuals should freely choose their marital partners, and families and outsiders should desist from intruding into their lives. In contrast, in the Indian society, most believe that one's family should determine partner choices and the focus of marriage should be the good of the family and community rather than the accomplishment of individual needs and desires.

The review also pointed to a gap in the literature with regard to the state of affairs in arranged marriages. While several studies indicated a high level of satisfaction in such marriages, equal or more forceful data showed that such marriages were marred by violence, abuses, and lack of freedom. Given these divergent data, the question was: How could marriages with high rates of violence, abuses, and discriminations against women account for high marital satisfaction? Seemingly some incongruity in the existing literature between the data on marital satisfaction and the current state of affairs in Indian arranged marriages exists. Aware of this issue, the current study explores the quality of marital relationship in arranged marriages.

Several family and marital researchers (e.g., Gottman and Gottman, 2008; Rusbult et al., 1998; Sternberg, 1986) developed and operationalized theoretical models and constructs that predict successful relationships and marriages. Most of this research is based on marriages of choice and other forms of dyadic relationships in the Western world, particularly in the United States (Allendorf and Ghimire, 2013). However, no consensus among these researchers about how marital or relationship quality should be measured exists. For example, should it be measured as one- or multi-dimensional construct? (Allendorf and Ghimire, 2013; Pimentel, 2000). There is no single standard measure that is used in all studies to assess relationship or marital quality (Allendorf and Ghimire, 2013). However, all generally accept that marital or relationship quality should refer to people's health and well-being in marriage (Allendorf and Ghimire, 2013). Health and well-being in marriage would mean that those relationships are characterized by a sense of bonding, caring, feeling of unity and companionship, mutual understanding, commitment, investment of resources, healthy interactions, and satisfactory emotional and sexual relationship (Gottman and Gottman, 2008; Hughes, 2007; Rusbult et al., 1998; Sternberg, 1986).

With this background of the literature on relationships, the researcher drew six variables from two of those models to serve as the conceptual framework for the current study on relationship quality in arranged marriages in India. The six variables are satisfaction, quality of alternatives, investment size, intimacy, passion, and commitment. These six variables were conceptualized as related to relationship quality in arranged marriages in India. The two theoretical models from which the six variables were drawn are the investment model (Rusbult et al., 1998) and the triangular theory of love (Sternberg, 1986). The following section will discuss these theories in detail and explain how these six variables will be used to assess relationship quality in arranged marriages in India.

THE INVESTMENT MODEL

The investment model proposed by Rusbult et al. (1998) is an extension of the interdependence theory, which was originally presented by Kelly and Thibaut (as cited in Rusbult et al., 1998). The developers of the interdependence theory argued that it is the need for dependence and not the personal disposition of partners that determined commitment and the consequent persistence in marital relationships. Partners feel a need to depend on each other. The strength of this dependence, according to the theory, is based on the level of satisfaction and the quality of alternatives. While recognizing and affirming the role of satisfaction and quality of alternatives in the development of dependence and commitment in a relationship, Rusbult et al. (1998) suggested that a third construct, *investment size*, was also important for it. That hypothesis gave rise to the development of the investment model. Figure 1 gives a graphic demonstration of this theory.

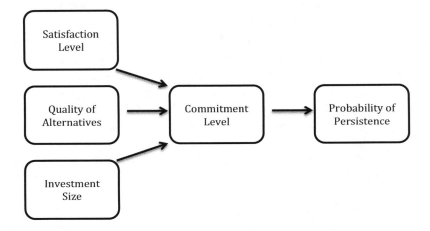

Figure 1. The Investment Model (Rusbult et al., 1998)

The three components of this model, satisfaction, quality of alternatives, and investments, are discussed in the following sections.

Satisfaction

The level of satisfaction "refers to the positive versus negative affect experienced in a relationship" (Rusbult et al., 1998, p. 3). The overall sense of satisfaction in a relationship (positive or negative) depends on the rewards and costs associated with the relationship (Etcheverry et al., 2012). If the outcomes from the relationship meet important needs or exceed the expectations, there is high satisfaction (Panayiotou, 2005). In other words, in relationships with high satisfaction, rewards are high and costs are few. For example, if Tom and his partner Becky fulfill each other's most important needs, which may include companionship, emotional and sexual pleasure, intellectual needs, so on and so forth, they may develop a positive feeling toward each other, and their satisfaction level may be higher. And because they help each other to experience a higher level of satisfaction they may want to depend on each other more. Their dependence on each other, in turn, helps growth in their commitment, persistence in marriage, and ultimately higher functioning in their marital relationship.

Bradbury et al. (2000), in their review of a decade's research on marital satisfaction, found that marital satisfaction was probably the single most important factor in understanding the quality of marriage. Rhyne's (1981) study shows that marital satisfaction is a multifaceted construct that pertains to areas such as love, friendship, sexual gratification, time spent with children, help at home, and treatment by in-laws. The interdependence theory and the investment model reiterate this fact that satisfaction plays a vital role in strengthening couples' marital commitment, persistence in marriage, and the overall higher functioning.

Quality of Alternatives

The quality of alternatives "refers to the perceived desirability of the best available alternative to a relationship" (Rusbult et al., 1998, p. 3). According to the interdependence theory and investment model, if a person has better alternatives outside the current relationship, his or her dependence on the partner will be less and consequently the commitment will be weaker. If alternatives are readily available, the person will not feel the need to depend on the partner, and consequently the commitment level will decline (Panayiotou, 2005). On the other hand, if the alternatives outside the current relationship are poorer, he or she will feel the need to depend on the partner more, and that will strengthen the commitment. In other words, if the desired outcomes are not available in other relationships, it means that there are fewer alternatives to the current relationship (Etcheverry et al., 2012). In that regard, the current relationship would be viewed as the best that would give the person the desired outcomes.

For example, if Tom finds his current relationship with Becky as the best available relationship to fulfill his needs and there are no better alternatives, his dependence on Becky will grow stronger, and that in turn will strengthen their commitment. The idea of poorer alternatives strengthening couples' dependence on each other is not in the sense of someone forced to stay in a relationship because of lack of choices or alternatives but rather in the sense of choosing the current relationship as the best relationship even when other alternatives are available. A person could have other alternatives (e.g., forming new relationship with another partner, the option of noninvolvement, depending on friends or family more), but the person deems the current relationship as the best over all other alternatives because it fulfills his or her important needs. Thus, according to the theory, the weaker the alternatives the better will be couples' commitment and quality of relationship.

Investments

Rusbult et al. (1998) argued that if satisfaction and quality of alternatives were the only reasons for people to persist in marriage, then a lot of marriages would break up when there is no more satisfaction and when there are better alternatives available outside of the relationship. But that is not the reality. There are marriages that persist in spite of low level of satisfaction or no satisfaction at all. There are also couples remaining married and committed to each other even when they have seemingly better alternatives available elsewhere. Hence, they argue that besides satisfaction and quality of alternatives, dependence and commitment are influenced by the size of each partner's investment in the relationship. By investment size the authors mean "the magnitude and importance of the resources that are attached to a relationship—resources that would decline in value or be lost if the relationship were to end" (Rusbult et al., 1998, p. 3). The theory suggests that because people invest a great deal into their relationships, it would be too costly and the desired outcomes would be lost if people were to end their relationships (Etcheverry et al., 2012; Panayiotou, 2005).

Partners in a marital relationship invest many resources, internal and external, direct and indirect, into the relationship with the belief that they would help to build the relationship. These resources would include the time, effort, and energy that partners put into the relationship. Visible and external resources that couples invest into their relationships would include bringing material and monetary resources to share with the partner, bringing one's own friends into the relationship allowing the partner to become friends with them, joining with the partner on a mutually agreeable plan of generating children, so on and so forth. Because they invest so much into the relationship, ending the relationship can be very costly and damaging.

So the authors argue that when partners invest so much into a relationship, it automatically works as a "psychological inducement" (Rusbult et al., 1998, p. 3) to depend on each other and persist in their relationship. An increased dependence on each other is thought to be helpful for an increase in their marital or relationship commitment. An increase in the commitment level consequently leads to persistence in the relationship and higher functioning.

As the authors predicted, the results of their study showed a significant positive correlation between commitment and satisfaction, a negative correlation between commitment and alternatives, and a positive correlation between commitment and investments (Rusbult et al., 1998). The study also affirmed that stronger commitment was indicative of higher functioning in relationships. Gender difference was another factor that stood out in the study. The study showed that in comparison to men, women had higher satisfaction, poorer alternative, greater investment, and stronger commitment.

The investment model is considered an appropriate framework to study a wide variety of populations and relationships (Macher, 2013; Panayiotou, 2005; Rodrigues and Lopes, 2013; Rusbult et al., 1998). The current study on the relationship quality in arranged marriages in India applied the basic constructs of this model in its exploration. Dependence, one of the basic constructs of the investment model, for example, is an all too familiar concept for the people in India. Social interdependence is a defining character of an Indian's life (Jacobson, 1996). When a person is born he or she is born into a family, a caste, a sub-caste, a clan, and a religious and linguistic community. Families and communities maintain strong networks of kinship and social ties. Jacobson describes this emphasis on the importance of social ties and interdependence in India well:

> In every activity, there is an assumption that social ties can help a person and that their absence can bring failure. Seldom do people carry out even the simplest task on their own.... A student applying to a college hopes that he has an influential relative or family friend who can put in a good word for him with the director of admissions. At the age of marriage, a young person expects that parents will take care of finding the appropriate bride or groom and arranging all the formalities. At the birth of a child, the new mother is assured that the child's kin will help her attend to the infant's needs. A businessman seeking to arrange a contract relies not only on his own abilities but also on the assistance of well-connected friends and relatives to help

finalize the deal. And finally, when facing death, a person is confi-
dent that offspring and other relatives will carry out the appropriate
funeral rites, including a commemorative feast when, through gifts
of clothing and food, continuing social ties are reaffirmed by all in
attendance. (p. 241)

Indians, in general, believe that their extended family would take
care of their physical, psychological, and financial needs (Medora, 2007).
Jacobson (1996) observed that because of this extreme interdependence,
people in India live with a sense of being part of and inseparable from these
groups, and their greatest fear may be the possibility of being left alone
without adequate social support to face the challenges of life. This feature
of interdependence is an organizing factor not only for the lives of individuals but also for couples in arranged marriages. As Jacobson (1996) and
Singh (2005) have noted, a marriage in India is a celebration of union not
only of the bride and the groom but also of two families, two cultures, or
two religions. According to the investment model, dependence plays a vital
role in couples' commitment, persistence, and higher functioning in marriage. Owing to the collectivistic and interdependent nature of the society,
dependence is a given in Indian arranged marriages. Persistence in such
marriages was reported to be high as well (Batabyal, 2001; Singh, 2005).
The present study explored the nature of the three variables of satisfaction,
quality of alternatives, and investments that contributed to commitment
and persistence in arranged marriages in India.

With regard to investment size, it was hard to say whether it was men
or women in India who invested more into the relationship. There have
been some studies on the level of satisfaction in arranged marriages in
India (e.g., Myers et al., 2005; Madathil and Benshoff, 2008; Yelsma and
Athappilly, 1988), but the quality of alternatives and investment size were
areas that were still largely unexplored. The investment model suggested
that persistence in relationship had to be preceded by a high level of commitment. A high level of commitment, Rusbult et al. (1998) noted, was a
good predictor of "overall couple adjustment" (p. 27) and higher functioning. Thus, to understand the overall quality of relationship in arranged
marriages in India, it was essential to examine the three antecedents of
dependence—that is, the level of satisfaction, quality of alternatives, and
investments.

THE TRIANGULAR THEORY OF LOVE

While the investment model tried to explain relationship quality in terms of satisfaction, alternatives, investments, and the consequent commitment, Sternberg (1986) proposed a somewhat closely related and yet different theory to explain relationship quality. According to his triangular theory of love, the ingredients of successful relationships are intimacy, passion, and commitment. These three ingredients, according to the theory, are like the three vertices of a triangle, and a balanced loving relationship is one in which all three of them are more or less equally matched. Both the investment model and the triangular theory of love have "commitment" as a common predictor of relationship quality. However, both theories differ in the way they understand the exact nature of commitment. In the investment model, commitment is an outcome of satisfaction, alternatives, and investments, whereas in the triangular theory of love, commitment is the continuation of the decision to stay and maintain the relationship. Figure 2 gives a graphic illustration of Sternberg's (1986) model.

Decision/Commitment

Figure 2. The Triangular Theory of Love Model (Sternberg, 1986)

The following section discusses the three ingredients proposed by the triangular theory of love, and explains how they offered a useful framework for the study of relationship quality in arranged marriages in India.

Intimacy

Intimacy refers to the feelings of closeness, bondedness, and connectedness that people experience in loving relationships (Sternberg, 1986). It gives rise to an experience of warmth in relationships, and it is largely dependent on the emotional investment of the persons in the relationship. Other authors such as Heller and Wood (2000) and Moore et al. (2001) also have defined intimacy in similar terms—that is, as a positive and affective relationship (understanding, validation, and caring) with one's significant other. Heller and Wood suggested that intimacy was a significant construct in solidifying couples' commitment, persistence in marriage, and the promotion of marital well-being and marital adjustment. In his research, Sternberg (1986) found that intimacy included experiences such as promotion of the welfare of the loved one, high regard for the loved one, giving and receiving of emotional support, and being able to count on the loved one in times of need. Overall, Sternberg found that intimacy was an essential component of loving relationships.

Passion

Passion refers to the drives that contribute to romance, physical attraction, and sexual consummation in loving relationships (Sternberg, 1986). It is an intense longing for union with the loved one. However, Sternberg noted, passion could be aroused by different kinds of needs. In a romantic relationship, the predominant need that arouses passion might be sexual union. In other circumstances, passion could be aroused by other needs such as those for self-esteem, nurturance, affiliation, dominance, submission, and self-actualization. According to Sternberg, the strength of these needs will vary across persons, situations, and kinds of relationships. Thus, the component of passion is largely dependent on the motivational involvement of the persons in the relationship. Passion is found to have a high positive correlation with relationship quality. In a study done by Fletcher et al. (2000) on relationship quality, the results supported this hypothesis. Sternberg (1986) observed that the component of passion would inevitably interact with the component of intimacy but they vary in the order of their development. For example, in a romantic relationship, passion may develop almost immediately and intimacy may develop only gradually. In a close friendship, on the other hand, intimacy may develop first and passion may develop only gradually. In any case, both these components are found to contribute largely to the formation of loving relationships.

Decision/Commitment

The decision/commitment component consists of two aspects: a decision to love someone and a commitment to maintain that love. The decision to love someone is a short-term aspect while the commitment to maintain that love is a long term one. In other words, a decision to love someone does not necessarily mean a commitment to maintain that love. The component of decision/commitment to love is largely dependent on the cognitive elements that are involved in the decision-making process. Referring to the role of decision and commitment in marriage, Sternberg (1986) suggested, "the institution of marriage represents a legalization of the commitment to a decision to love another throughout one's life" (p. 123).

The three components of love, intimacy, passion, and commitment interact with one another in many ways in a relationship (Sternberg, 1986). If the passion component is emphasized in the relationship over the other two, the physical attraction is likely to play a larger role than intimacy and decision/commitment. If the intimacy component is emphasized over the other two, the lovers are more likely to function as good friends, and the physical and the commitment aspects may be marginal. If the decision/commitment component is emphasized over intimacy and passion, a high level of commitment and a low level of physical attraction and intimacy may characterize the relationship. The importance and the intensity of these components also vary from one relationship to the other. For example, one could be involved in an intimate relationship with one's parents, siblings, a close friend, and a lover, but passionately involved only in a romantic relationship with his or her lover. The passion component may play a larger role in short-term relationships, while the intimacy and decision/commitment components may have a bigger role to play in long-term relationships. In some relationships, commitment can arise out of one's passionate and intimate involvement with another person, but in others, commitment can contribute to the development of intimate involvement and passionate arousal.

When applied to marital relationships, the theory suggests that a loving and affective relationship between partners becomes possible when there is a large amount of love in terms of intimacy, passion, and commitment, and when partners are able and willing to match these three components of love. A perfect match of the three components may be an unrealistic goal, but according to Sternberg (1986), one of the ways to assess whether or not the components are balanced is to take into account how partners express their love in all these three areas. "Without expression," Sternberg opined, "even the greatest of loves can die" (p. 132).

For each of the three components, Sternberg identified certain "love-action/expression" behaviors. The expression of intimacy will consist of lovers communicating with each other their inner feelings, promoting each other's well-being, sharing each other's possessions, time, and self, expressing empathy for each other, and offering emotional and material support to each other. The expression of passion will consist of lovers engaging in kissing, hugging, gazing, touching, and making love. The expression of decision/commitment will consist of lovers pledging their commitment and fidelity to each other, staying in the relationship through hard times, and deciding to get engaged and married.

Sternberg (1986) suggested that considering the fact that one does not have a choice of one's partner in arranged marriages the three components of love might be highly imbalanced at the beginning of such relationships. In such marriages, intimacy and passion may be very marginal while decision/commitment may be overemphasized at the beginning of the relationship. However, decision/commitment could be a generator of intimacy and passion in the course of time. In any case, for a marital relationship to be healthy, happy, and loving, the three components of intimacy, passion, and decision/commitment have to be more or less equally matched. The current study explored whether these three components of love characterized the relationships in arranged marriages in India.

The six variables of satisfaction, quality of alternatives, investments, intimacy, passion, and commitment that we discussed above were hypothesized to be associated with the relationship quality in arranged marriages in India. Also, the current study explored the gender difference in all the study variables. Rusbult et al. (1998) had found in their study gender differences in the outcome variable. In comparison with men, women had stronger commitment, higher satisfaction, poorer alternatives, and greater investment. Rhyne's (1981) study on marital satisfaction among married Canadians showed that men were generally more satisfied with their marriage than women. Given these findings about marriages of choice and other dyadic relationships in the Western world, the current study examined whether there were gender differences with regard to any of the study variables concerning arranged marriages in India.

HYPOTHESES

Based on the theoretical models discussed above and following up on the research questions stated at the end of Part I, the following hypotheses were formulated for the current study:

Hypothesis 1: The respondents' marital satisfaction shows a significant positive correlation with their relationship quality.

Hypothesis 2: The respondents' quality of alternatives shows a significant negative correlation with their relationship quality.

Hypothesis 3: The investment of resources in the respondents' marriage shows a significant positive correlation with their relationship quality.

Hypothesis 4: Intimacy in the respondents' marital relationship shows a significant positive correlation with their relationship quality.

Hypothesis 5: Passion in the respondents' marital relationship shows a significant positive correlation with their relationship quality.

Hypothesis 6: Commitment in the respondents' marital relationship shows a significant positive correlation with their relationship quality.

Hypothesis 7: The added factors of marital satisfaction, quality of alternatives, investments, intimacy, passion, and commitment in the respondents' marriage show a significant relationship with their relationship quality.

Hypothesis 8: There is a significant difference between men and women in their assessment of relationship quality, satisfaction, quality of alternatives, investments, intimacy, passion, and commitment.

PART III

Methodology

7

The Design of the Current Study

RESEARCH HAS GENERALLY BEEN done in two distinct ways, quantitatively and qualitatively (Barnes, 2012; Bartholomew and Brown, 2012; Terrell, 2012). Quantitative researchers collect numerical data from participants and statistically analyze them to study the phenomenon of their inquiry, whereas qualitative researchers seek to understand the phenomenon as it is understood and experienced by the participants in the natural setting of their lives (Arghode, 2012; Hill, 2006; Hoe and Hoare, 2012; Farrelly, 2013). Mixed methods research emerged as a way to integrate these two methodologies and provided researchers a new way to "develop rich insights into various phenomena of interest that cannot be fully understood using only a quantitative or a qualitative method" (Venkatesh et al., 2013, p. 21). In mixed methods research, the researcher uses both quantitative and qualitative methods in a single study to collect and analyze data, integrate the findings, and draw inferences (Barnes, 2012; Bartholomew and Brown, 2012; Venkatesh et al., 2013; Wisdom et al., 2012). In recent years, mixed methods research has been widely used in areas such as nursing, psychology, education, sociology, information systems, political science, family therapy, and other human sciences (Bradley and Johnson, 2005; Nelson and Allred, 2005; Terrell, 2012; Venkatesh et al., 2013).

The purpose of the current study was to explore the phenomenon of relationship quality in arranged marriages in India, and mixed methods research was conceived as the best methodology for determining the same. The reason for using this method was to "develop rich insights" (Venkatesh et al., 2013, p. 21) regarding the relationship quality in arranged marriages in India. Arranged marriages in India are a complex phenomenon and a combination of both quantitative and qualitative methods was considered a better approach to study it. Wisdom et al. (2012) highlighted this advantage of doing mixed methods when they suggested that "mixed methods can be a better approach to research than either quantitative-only or qualitative-only methods when a single data source is not sufficient to understand the topic" (p. 722).

In the present study, the quantitative phase gave the researcher numerical data about the different dimensions of the participants' relationship quality. In the qualitative phase, listening to the participants in one-on-one, face-to-face interviews helped the non-quantifiable aspects about their relationship to emerge. Open-ended questions gave opportunities for the participants to express more freely their thoughts and feelings about their marital relationship. Thus, the participants had an opportunity to describe the level of their relationship quality not only in numbers but also in words. The interviews also elicited responses that were unrelated to the quantitative measures. Thus, a combination of both methods was a better approach to capture the experience of the participants.

THE CONCURRENT TRIANGULATION DESIGN

The current study on the relationship quality in arranged marriages in India used the concurrent triangulation design, whereby both quantitative and qualitative data were collected concurrently (Creswell, 2009; Terrell, 2012). The ideal practice in such a design is to give both the quantitative and qualitative methods equal weight (Creswell, 2009). The current study followed this rule. Using multiple instruments, the researcher collected quantitative data on the participants' level of marital satisfaction, investment of resources, quality of alternatives, commitment, intimacy, passion, and the overall quality of relationship. Using an open-ended interview guide, the researcher concurrently gathered qualitative data through one-on-one, face-to-face interviews with a small sample of these participants. The data obtained from both the quantitative and qualitative phases were analyzed separately, and then the results were compared to determine whether "there is convergence, differences, or some combination" (Creswell, 2009, p. 213). The following diagram illustrates the concurrent triangulation design that was used in the current study.

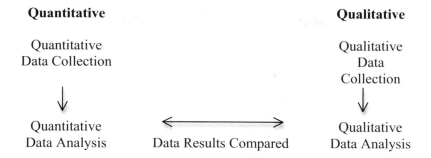

Quantitative   **Qualitative**

Figure 3. The Concurrent Triangulation Design

To recruit participants for the study, the researcher used both convenience sampling and snowball sampling techniques. First, the researcher
sought permission and cooperation from the University of Mysore, which is
located in South India, to do the study. Using a convenience sampling tech-
nique, the researcher then established contact with third parties (Bourque
and Fielder, 2003), such as community leaders and heads of educational institutions and social service agencies in the two states of Kerala and Karnataka in India, who helped to spread the word about the research. The third
parties posted the participant recruitment fliers and made announcements
to their congregation or communities about the current research, helping
the researcher to identify prospective participants from their communities
or agencies who were readily available for the study (Gould, 2002). The researcher then went to the respective sites of the third parties on a mutually
convenient date, met the prospective subjects who were readily available
for the study, and distributed to them self-administered questionnaires.

Considering the researcher might not be able to obtain the required
number of subjects for the study, he used snowball sampling. The researcher
requested that subjects "identify others who might qualify as respondents"
(Rea and Parker, 2005, p. 173). The researcher went to the respective sites
of the third parties again to meet those who responded to the request of
the subjects, and distributed to them self-administered questionnaires.
The recruitment statement to prospective participants was enclosed in the
questionnaire packet.

The main criteria for the participation in this study were that the
subjects were willing to participate in this study without any coercion,
they were eighteen years old or above, they were able to understand and
speak English, they were currently living in an arranged marriage, they had

completed at least one year in their marriage at the time of this study, and they were not close friends or family members of the researcher.

Only individuals in arranged marriages were chosen for the study as there are semi-arranged marriages and marriages of choice in India (Singh, 2005), and the focus of this study was specifically on arranged marriages. The reason for excluding persons who were married for less than a year was based on the assumption that it might take at least one year for couples in arranged marriages to get to know each other and move toward solidifying their relationship (Chekki, 1996). Only individuals who had attained the legal status of an adult according to the Indian law, which is eighteen years of age, were selected for the study for the specific reason of being able to consent freely to the study. The decision to restrict the study to individuals who were fluent in English only was a pragmatic decision in consideration of the limited time and resources available to the researcher. The difficulties and challenges involved in getting the participants' responses translated into English if they responded in languages other than English are enormous and time consuming, and such elaborate processes were beyond the scope of the current study. The prospective participants were adequately informed of these criteria in the recruitment statement that was given to them. Participants were not compensated monetarily or by way of any gifts.

PARTICIPANTS

The study took place in India, specifically in the two southern states of Kerala and Karnataka. The participants were all Indians who are currently living in arranged marriages in India.

To compute the sample size, the researcher used the G*Power 3.1 program developed by Faul et al. (2009). G*Power is "a stand-alone power analysis program for many statistical tests commonly used in the social, behavioral, and bio-medical sciences" (Faul et al., 2009, p. 1149). The program helps researchers to compute the necessary sample size according to the specified values for the required significance level (α), the desired statistical power ($1-\beta$), the preferred effect size ($f2$), and the number of predictors. Setting the alpha at .05, the statistical power at .95, the effect size at .25, and the number of predictors at six, the sample size calculated for the current study was ninety. However, according to Bourque and Fielder (2003), "sample loss" (p. 154) is a serious matter to consider when deciding on the sample size. These authors noted that sample loss could occur if "individuals decline to participate, group turnout is lower than expected, or the materials are not distributed as directed" (p. 154). In some surveys, the authors noted, the response rate could be as low as 20 percent. Thus, the expected non-response rate is a legitimate reason to increase the sample size. Additionally, in social sciences, because researchers usually study indirect, ambiguous attitudes and beliefs of people, the sample size determined based on analysis estimates is often found to be inadequate. The analysis estimates might indicate what is minimally necessary for analyses, but that may not necessarily be sufficient. Howell (2010) noted that large samples are required to obtain "a reasonable amount of power" (p. 534). To address such concerns, the best approach suggested by researchers is to increase the sample size to a level that is deemed fit. Hence, for the current study, the sample size was increased, making the total of expected participants three hundred. A very good response rate was obtained. Out of the 400 questionnaire packets distributed, 287 were returned. This amounted to a 72 percent return rate. This is a very high response rate, considering what Bourque and Fielder (2003) have stated, a response rate in some surveys as low as 20 percent.

The most important guiding principle in qualitative studies for determining sample size is the concept of saturation—that is, reaching a point where no new information or data emerges from interviews (Mason, 2010). Since the point of saturation cannot be determined in advance, sample sizes differ from one study to the other. However, Mason, in his review of several PhD studies that used qualitative interviews, found that the most common sample sizes were ten, twenty, twenty-five, thirty, and forty. Due to the limitations of time and resources, the current study set the sample size for the qualitative phase at ten, with the decision to increase or decrease the number depending on how soon the researcher reached the point of saturation.

Through the recruitment statement as well as during the distribution of the questionnaires, the researcher informed the subjects about the one-on-one, face-to-face qualitative interviews that they were invited to volunteer for. If they were willing to participate in the interviews, they could indicate their willingness by checking a box at the end of the survey and provide their contact information on a separate sheet of paper and enclose it in the completed questionnaire packet. They could also contact the researcher by email or telephone and express their willingness to participate in the interviews.

The participants were informed that if they volunteered for the interviews, they would be contacted in the order the completed questionnaires were received. They were also told that if the researcher did not contact them for the interviews, their contact information would be destroyed. Out of the 287 individuals who completed and returned the questionnaire packets, forty-eight individuals volunteered for the follow-up interviews and provided their contact information. Although the sample size for the qualitative interviews was set at ten, it took fourteen interviews to reach the point of saturation. Accordingly, the fourteen subjects who returned the completed questionnaires first were contacted. The researcher conducted one-on-one, face-to-face phenomenological interviews with them at a time and a place that were convenient to them. Their contact information was retained for the purpose of member checking, while the contact information of the remaining volunteers was destroyed.

The sample for the current study had several unique characteristics. In many of the studies found in the literature, the samples often consist of undergraduate university students from a particular field of study (e.g., Etcheverry et al., 2012; Pistole et al., 2010; Rusbult et al., 1998). In contrast, the subjects in the current study came from a variety of backgrounds. They were young and old. Ages of the participants ranged from twenty-one to seventy. The mean age of the participants was 39.21. Out of the 287 participants, 220 (76.7 percent) were women and sixty-seven (23.3 percent) were men. Among those who volunteered and participated in the qualitative interviews, nine were women (64.3 percent) and five were men (35.7 percent).

They were a diverse group of people of different religions, including Christians (48 percent), Hindus (47 percent), and Muslims (5 percent). They also varied in their duration of marriage, with the length of marriages ranging from one year to a high of forty-four years. Most of the participants, 87 percent, were employed, working in a variety of fields. Roughly 60 percent of the participants were teachers. Additionally, there were also business people, doctors, nurses, engineers, bankers, managers, accountants, and administrators. All the participants were educated, with 92 percent of them having a bachelor's degree or higher. About 70 percent of the subjects belonged to the high-income group. The other 30 percent came from the low or middle income classes. All the subjects came from the urban setting. Thus, the sample participants possessed a rich combination of backgrounds. See Table 1 for an overview of the participant characteristics.

Table 1: Participant Demographics

Total No. of Participants	287						
Gender	Male: 67 (23.3 percent)				Female: 220 (76.7 percent)		
Age	Mean 39.21	Median 37	Mode 32	SD 10.250	Range 49	Min. 21	Max. 70
Religion	Christian: 139 (48 percent)		Hindu: 134 (47 percent)		Muslim: 14 (5 percent)		
Duration of Marriage	Mean 13.48	Median 11	Mode 10	SD 9.804	Range 43	Min. 1	Max. 44
Employment Status	Yes = 86 percent				No = 14 percent		
Occupation	Teacher: 59.9 percent		Business: 3.5 percent		Manager: 3.5 percent		
	Nurse: 1.7 percent		Engineer: 2.1 percent		Banker: 2.8 percent		
	Govt. Employee: 2.8 percent		Technician: 4.2 percent		Others: 19.5 percent		
Family Income	Low: 10 percent		Medium: 18 percent		High: 70 percent		
Level of Education	Completed High School: 8 percent			Bachelor's or higher: 92 percent			

RESEARCHER'S ROLE

The researcher's presence in the lives of the participants of a study may be relatively brief, but his or her cultural background, societal status, predispositions, experiences, beliefs, values, and biases have a great influence on how he or she reviews the related literature, and understands, analyzes, and interprets the data. Due to this reason, Speziale and Carpenter (2007) suggested that researchers should set aside, as much as possible, their prejudgments, suppositions, biases, and preconceived ideas about the problem (phenomenon) that is being investigated. Husserl called this process the "epoche" or bracketing (Moustakas, 1994). Bracketing or the epoche allows the researcher to look at the phenomenon with a fresh and unbiased mindset. Epoche does not eliminate or doubt everything, but only the knowing of things in advance (Moustakas, 1994).

The process of epoche or bracketing was very significant for the current study, particularly in view of the qualitative phase of the research. Because the researcher is an Indian and the current study is on arranged marriages in India, there might have been many things that were common between the participants of the study and the researcher. Also, there might have been many differences between the participants and the researcher in regard to the cultural, developmental, religious, and social backgrounds (Speziale and Carpenter, 2007). Hence, it is important to place a brief account of my biography before the readers so that the current study could be understood in the backdrop of this background.

I am a brown-eyed, light complexioned male Catholic, born and raised in the state of Kerala, India. I am the youngest of four children, and my parents, both of whom are deceased, had an arranged marriage. As I can recall, at least 95 percent of my family and people in the neighborhood have had arranged marriage as the norm. I have traveled far and wide, both within and outside India. As I moved out of my home state, Kerala, I came across other cultures and societies where marriage and marital relationships had varieties of meanings, practices, and implications. Nevertheless, my thoughts and ideas about arranged marriages are still intimately linked to my experience of the family system and marital practices in India. Although I have been away from India for the past eight years (at the time of this research) for the purpose of work and study in the United States, I still consider myself an "insider" when it comes to things concerning the life and culture of Indians. Recognizing all these factors, it was my top priority to set aside my preconceived ideas and biases about couples and arranged marriages in India and conduct the current study without the interference of any such bias. To ensure the rigor and trustworthiness of the study, I made use of processes such as "member checking" and "auditing." These two processes are discussed later.

8

The Quantitative Phase

STRATEGY: SURVEY METHOD

THE CURRENT STUDY ON arranged marriages in India used the survey method to collect quantitative data from the participants. "A survey design," according to Creswell (2009), "provides a quantitative or numeric description of trends, attitudes, or opinions of a population by studying a sample of that population. From sample results, the researcher generalizes or makes claims about the population" (p. 145). In a survey, the participants are presented with one or a set of questionnaires, which they complete and return to the researcher (Reitz and Anderson, 2013). In the current study, the measures that the participants were asked to complete consisted of a demographic information questionnaire (see Appendix A), the Relationship Assessment Scale (see Appendix B), three subscales of the Investment Model Scale (see Appendix C), three subscales of the Triangular Love Scale (see Appendix D), and a single-item questionnaire about the overall relationship quality in marriage (see Appendix E).

PROCEDURE

After the third parties posted the research recruitment fliers and made announcements to their congregation or community about the current research, the researcher went to the respective sites of the third parties on a mutually convenient date to distribute the questionnaire packet to the prospective subjects who were readily available for the study. The questionnaire packet consisted of a set of self-administered questionnaires, the recruitment statement, and a letter of instructions. The subjects were asked to use paper-and-pencil techniques to complete the questionnaires in a semi-supervised administration environment (Bourque and Fielder, 2003). It was a semi-supervised administration as the subjects completed the questionnaires at a time and place that was convenient to them. According to Bourque and Fielder, self-administered questionnaires could be completed in a variety of ways and situations. One of the ways is to do it in a semi-supervised situation where questionnaires are distributed to prospective participants by the researcher or his or her representatives and the participants complete them in a place and at a time that is convenient to them. In such a process, the researcher or his or her representative does not give any formal presentation of instructions to the prospective respondents as a group, but "rather, each respondent receives pertinent instructions when he or she is given the questionnaire" (Bourque and Fielder, 2003, p. 6). In the current study, although the packet containing the questionnaires contained a set of instructions for the participants, the researcher gave a few pertinent instructions to the participants. The completion of the questionnaires was expected to take 25–30 minutes.

Since the respondents self-administered the questionnaires they could "answer the questions at their own pace" (Reitz and Anderson, 2013, p. 23). However, the researcher was available to answer questions by telephone and e-mail.

Through the recruitment statement, the researcher explained to the subjects the nature, purpose, and requirements of the study that they were undertaking, and sought their consent. The completion of the survey was taken as an indication that they had agreed to and expressed informed consent to complete the survey and be subjects in the current research. The subjects who completed the questionnaires were asked not to write their name or any other identifying information anywhere on the completed questionnaire packet. However, since the subjects who completed the questionnaires had an opportunity to be selected for one-on-one, face-to-face interviews with the researcher, complete anonymity of all the participants was not possible in this study. If they were selected for the phenomenological interviews, the participants were assured that their names or identifying information would not be included in the final analysis and reports. They were also assured that if the results of this study were published in scientific research journals, presented at professional conferences, or published in a book like this, all identifying information about them would be excluded from all such reports or presentations. The participants were also informed that they were free to stop or withdraw from the study at any time, for any personal reasons. Other than the risks of loss of time, boredom, and fatigue in completing the questionnaires, there was no harm or emotional trauma involved for the subjects in participating in this study

Upon the completion of the questionnaires, the subjects were given several options to get the completed questionnaires back to the researcher. They could directly send it or bring it to the researcher's address in India, which was provided in the recruitment statement. After sealing the envelope, they could also drop it in a secure, locked box that was placed at each of the sites by the researcher. The secure locked box was in a locked office at each of the sites. These options were mentioned in the recruitment statement. The researcher instructed the third parties not to open the envelope or the locked box. Only the researcher had direct contact with the completed questionnaires, and these were kept in a locked, secure cabinet in a locked office that only the researcher had access to.

MEASURES

The measures that the participants were asked to complete consisted of a demographic information questionnaire, the Relationship Assessment Scale (RAS), three subscales of the Investment Model Scale (IMS), three subscales of the Triangular Love Scale (TLS), and a single-item questionnaire about the overall relationship quality in marriage.

Demographic Information Schedule

The demographic information schedule consisted of items such as gender, age, religion, duration of marriage, employment status, occupation, economic status, and level of education. Personal information, such as names that revealed the identity of the participants, was not part of the demographic information schedule.

Relationship Assessment Scale (RAS)

The Relationship Assessment Scale (RAS) (Hendrick, 1988, 2000; Corcoran and Fischer, 2000) was used to measure the dependent variable of relationship quality in arranged marriages in India. The RAS is an instrument designed to measure an individual's sense of the quality of relationship with his or her partner. The instrument helps a clinician or researcher to obtain a good estimate of an individual's relationship quality. The brevity of the measure makes it easy to be administered and scored. The instrument has been proved suitable to assess multiple types of relationships (Renshaw et al., 2010). The RAS has also been used in research in various fields, including family therapy (Rask et al., 2010).

The RAS is a seven-item five-point Likert-type scale with scores ranging from one (low relationship quality) to five (high relationship quality). Items four and seven are reverse-scored. Scores over 4.0 would indicate lack of distress in relationships, whereas scores closer to 3.5 for men and between 3.5 and 3.0 for women would indicate greater distress in relationships (Hendrick et al., 1998). The total score ranges from seven (low relationship quality) to thirty-five (high relationship quality), which means that scores over twenty-eight would indicate lack of distress in relationships or high relationship quality. Sample items in the scale are, "How well does your partner meet your needs?" and "How much do you love your partner?"

The RAS has demonstrated satisfactory psychometric properties in terms of its validity and reliability (Rask et al., 2010). Hendrick (1988) conducted two studies for this purpose. In the first study, 235 undergraduate students (118 males, 117 females) were administered the RAS and other measures of relationship. Since some of them did not meet the full criteria of the study, responses from only 125 of these students were retained for the final analysis. The RAS showed "impressive correlation" (Hendrick, 1988, p. 95) with other measures of relationship. The correlations between the items in the RAS scale were moderate. In the second study, the RAS and other measures of relationship, including the Dyadic Adjustment Scale (DAS; Spanier, 1976), a widely used satisfaction instrument, were administered to 57 dating couples (114 subjects). As in the first study, the RAS demonstrated good validity with significant correlations with several measures of relationship. The scale also showed good reliability with an alpha of .86. The RAS had a correlation of .80 with the DAS (Hendrick et al., 1998).

Hendrick et al. (1998) did additional studies further demonstrating strong psychometric properties for the scale. Accordingly, studies of the RAS were conducted on a variety of samples such as married couples, dating couples, and clinical couples or couples in treatment (Hendrick et al.,

1998). In studies of married couples, the scores ranged from 4.05 to 4.37. The alpha for the RAS was .93. In studies of dating couples, men reported a satisfaction level of 4.30, and women reported 4.33, with standard deviations less than 1.00. The alpha for the RAS was .73. In the use of the RAS for clinical couples, the score of satisfaction for women was 3.27, with a standard deviation of 1.03, and for men it was 3.66, with a standard deviation of .87. Thus, overall, for non-clinical couples, scores ranged from 4.05 to 4.37, and for clinical couples, the scores ranged from 3.27 for women to 3.66 for men.

Hendrick et al. (1998) computed correlations between the RAS and the DAS, and the results showed that the RAS had high correlation with the DAS (.80 in one study and .88 in another study). The correlation with the Kansas Marital Satisfaction Scale (KMS; Schumm et al., 1986), another frequently used measure of relationship satisfaction, was also high, with .64 for men and .74 for women in one study.

In recent years, several researchers have used the RAS (Ireland et al., 2010; Klumb et al., 2006; Malinen et al., 2010; Rask et al., 2010; Renshaw et al., 2010; Salvatore et al., 2011; Slatcher and Pennebaker, 2006). All of them found this scale desirable, easy to administer, and appropriate to measure relationship quality. For example, in a longitudinal study on recovery from conflict in romantic relationships, Salvatore et al. (2011) administered the RAS to the participants, and asked them to rate their satisfaction with their current partner and the relationship. The results indicated that having a partner who is better able to recover from conflict was associated with experiencing greater satisfaction and more positive relationship emotions.

For the current study, RAS was preferred to other measures of relationship quality because of its brevity, its ability to assess different dimensions of relationships, and the ease in its administration. Although the DAS is a widely used instrument on relationship satisfaction, it is lengthier and more cumbersome to administer than the RAS (Hendrick et al., 1998). Likewise, although the KMS is brief and easy to administer, all the three items in it refer to satisfaction, whereas the items in RAS refer to other components of relationship as well (Hendrick et al., 1998). These authors suggested that RAS would be a good scale for researchers who are trying to assess different dimensions of relationship. But most of all, the RAS is found to be an appropriate measure for a wide array of partnered relationships (Hendrick et al., 1998). Hence, this scale was preferred to other measures for the study on the relationship quality in arranged marriages in India.

Investment Model Scale (IMS; Satisfaction, Alternatives, and Investment)

According to the investment model, three variables—satisfaction, alternatives, and investments—are associated with commitment in relationships, and commitment, in turn, leads to persistence and higher functioning in relationships (Rusbult et al., 1998). The three subscales of satisfaction, quality of alternatives, and investment size in the Investment Model Scale were used in the current study on arranged marriages in India.

Each of the three subscales of satisfaction, quality of alternatives, and investment size has two types of items, a five-item facet section and a five-item global section. According to Rusbult et al. (1998), participants might find it difficult to answer global items without adequate illustration. Facet items provide that illustration, and they enhance participants' comprehensibility of global items. However, in the final analysis, only the global items are included (Rusbult et al., 1998). An example of facet items for the subscale of satisfaction is, "My partner fulfills my needs for intimacy (sharing personal thoughts, secrets, etc.)." An example of facet items for quality of alternatives is, "My needs for intimacy (sharing personal thoughts, secrets, etc.) could be fulfilled in alternative relationships." An example of facet items for investment size is, "I have invested a great deal of time in our relationship." The responses to facet items range from "don't agree at all" to "agree completely."

After each of the facet sections, participants rate a five-item global subscale. An example of global items for satisfaction subscale is, "I feel satisfied with our relationship." An example of global items for quality of alternatives is, "The people other than my partner with whom I might become involved are very appealing." An example of global items for investment size is, "I have put a great deal into our relationship that I would lose if the relationship were to end." The global subscales use a nine-point Likert-type scale with scores ranging from zero (do not agree at all) to eight (agree completely). For the current study, this scoring was changed into one to nine (keeping the same response pattern) to make it consistent with other scales used in the study and thus making it easier for the participants. This change in the scoring pattern was made based on the recommendations of Rusbult et al., in using the instrument. The authors suggested that since the RAS had obtained good validity and reliability in researches examining multiple types of relationships, it was "desirable to tailor the instrument to the population under consideration" (Rusbult et al., 1998, p. 384) by making the necessary changes.

Higher scores on the satisfaction subscale would indicate a higher level of satisfaction, resulting in greater commitment. Likewise, higher scores on the investment size subscale would indicate a higher level of investment, resulting in greater commitment. Higher scores on the alternatives subscale would indicate higher level of alternatives, resulting in lower commitment.

Rusbult et al. (1998) conducted three studies to examine the validity and reliability of the scale. In the first study, the participants consisted of 415 undergraduates (243 women, 172 males) enrolled in an introductory psychology course at the University of North Carolina at Chapel Hill. In the second study, the participants consisted of 326 undergraduate students. And in the third study, the participants consisted of 186 undergraduate students. The participants in all three studies were in dating relationships. The analyses of the three studies revealed good reliability for the global items of each of the subscales. Alphas ranged from .92 to .95 for the satisfaction subscale, .82 to .88 for quality of alternatives, and .82 to .84 for investment size. All three studies provided evidence for the convergent, discriminant, and predictive validity of the instrument.

Supporting evidence for convergent and discriminant validity, analyses showed that each facet measure was more powerfully correlated with its corresponding global measure than with the global measures of other constructs. Revealing evidence for predictive validity, regression analyses showed that the three factors of satisfaction, alternatives, and investment collectively predicted commitment level ($R2s$ ranged from .69 to .77; all ps < .01). In other words, commitment level was significantly positively correlated with satisfaction (betas ranged from –.47 to .69), negatively correlated with alternatives (betas ranged from –.29 to –.32), and positively correlated with investments (betas ranged from .19 to .27). The analyses showed only a moderate collinearity among satisfaction, alternatives, and investment. Analyses revealed that the three variables were moderately associated with other measures of relationship quality such as the Dyadic Adjustment Scale (Spanier, 1976) and Inclusion of Other in the Self (IOS; Aron et al., 1992). In addition, the analyses showed that in comparison to men, women exhibited higher satisfaction, lower quality of alternatives, and greater investment, all of which lead to stronger commitment.

In several other studies (Etcheverry et al., 2013; Macher, 2013; Pistole et al., 2010; Rodrigues and Lopes, 2013; Vanderdrift et al., 2012), the findings of Rusbult et al. (1998) have been well replicated. In a study of long-distance versus geographically close relationships, Pistole et al. (2010)

found that Cronbach's alpha reliabilities were .94 for satisfaction, .85 for alternatives, and .83 for investments. High satisfaction contributed to commitment in both long-distance and geographically close relationships. High investments were salient in long-distance relationships. And low alternatives were salient in geographically close relationships. In the study done by Vanderdrift et al. on commitment in friends with benefits relationships, results showed that satisfaction, investment, and alternatives were predictive of commitment. The three subscales evidenced acceptable reliability (satisfaction, $r = .90$; investment, $r = .85$; alternatives, $r = .76$).

The three subscales of satisfaction, alternatives, and investment have proven to be strong predictors for higher functioning in relationships. The current study used these subscales along with others to examine the association of these variables with relationship quality in arranged marriages in India.

Triangular Love Scale (TLS; Commitment, Intimacy, and Passion)

Sternberg's (1986) triangular theory of love posits that the ingredients of a successful relationship are intimacy, passion, and commitment. The current study on the relationship quality in arranged marriages in India used the three subscales of intimacy, passion, and commitment in Sternberg's Triangular Love Scale (Sternberg, 1986, 1990, 1997).

The Triangular Love Scale is a forty-five-item, nine-point Likert-type scale in which the scores range from one (not at all) to nine (extremely). The middle point, five, represents "moderately." The scale measures an individual's level of intimacy, passion, and commitment in his or her relationship. Higher scores indicate greater intimacy, passion, and commitment (Cusack et al., 2012). An example of items in the intimacy subscale is, "I have a warm relationship with _____." An example of items in the passion subscale is, "Just seeing _____ excites me." An example of items in the commitment subscale is, "I am committed to maintaining my relationship with _____."

The scale has sound psychometric properties. To test the construct validity of the scale, Sternberg (1997) conducted two studies. In the first study, the participants consisted of 84 adults with equal number of men and women, and in the second study, 101 adults (50 men and 51 women) participated. In the second study, Sternberg used a revised version of the scale with each of the subscales having fifteen items. In Study 1, he had only twelve items. The number of items was increased to obtain sound psychometric properties. With regard to internal and construct validity, the result in both studies indicated that the intimacy, passion, and commitment subscales served their function quite well. In the computation of the external validity, Sternberg (1997) found that the Triangular Love Scale and Rubin's (1970) Love Scale and Liking Scale were highly correlated. The results also showed that Sternberg's scale was more predictive of relationship satisfaction than Rubin scales (Study 1: 0.59 for the Rubin Love Scale, 0.36 for the Rubin Liking Scale, and 0.86, 0.77, and 0.75 respectively for the Sternberg intimacy, passion, and commitment scales; Study 2: 0.59 and 0.56 for the Rubin love scale, 0.56 for the Rubin liking scale, and 0.76, 0.76, and 0.67 for the Sternberg intimacy, passion, and commitment scales respectively). The overall reliabilities for the TLS were high (α = .93 to α = .95; intimacy = 0.90, passion = 0.80, commitment = 0.80). The one shortcoming of the scale was that when the intercorrelations of intimacy, passion, and commitment were computed, the correlations were shown to be relatively high. The overall correlations were 0.61 for passion and intimacy, 0.72 for passion and commitment, and 0.73 for intimacy and commitment (Sternberg, 1997).

In several other studies (Chojnacki and Walsh, 1990; Cusack et al., 2012; Hendrick and Hendrick, 1989; Madey and Rodgers, 2009; Ng and Cheng, 2010; Panayiotou, 2005), Sternberg's (1986) findings about the TLS have been replicated. In some studies (e.g., Overbreek et al., 2007), the scale's divergent validity was established. In a study of 90 students (45 men and 45 women) who were in dating relationships, Chojnacki and Walsh (1990) found results confirming the findings of Sternberg. The tests were administered twice with a gap of two weeks in between. At both administrations, Cronbach alpha coefficients were in the .90s for each subscale and for the overall measure, indicating high internal consistency. The results also indicated concurrent validity. The overall test-retest reliability correlation for the scale was .79 (passion = .81, intimacy = .75, and decision/commitment = .77). Again, administering the TLS and other measures on love to a sample of 424 undergraduate students at a southwestern university in the United States, Hendrick and Hendrick (1989) found that the total forty-five-item Triangular Love Scale had an alpha of .97, the subscale alphas ranged from .93 to .96, and the interscale correlations ranged from .71 to .78. In both these studies, Chojnacki and Walsh (1990) and Hendrick and Hendrick (1989) found that the interscale correlations were generally high.

Administering the TLS to a sample of fifty-five university undergraduate students, Madey and Rodgers (2009) found that intimacy, passion, and commitment highly correlated with the relationship satisfaction score. With the aim of examining the psychometric properties of an adolescent version of Sternberg's TLS, Overbreek et al. (2007) administered the instrument to 435 adolescents aged twelve to eighteen years in the Netherlands. The results indicated that the scale was a highly reliable measure with satisfactory convergent validity (intimacy: $r = .49$, $p = .001$; passion: $r = .24$, $p = .001$; commitment: $r = .39$, $p = .001$) and good divergent validity. The results also indicated adequate construct validity for the scale. Intimacy, passion, and commitment were positively correlated with relationship satisfaction (Overbreek et al., 2007).

The scale has been used in different relationship types and cultural settings too. In a study of 90 lesbians and 213 heterosexual women, Cusack et al. (2012) administered Sternberg's TLS to examine whether intimacy, passion, and commitment were predictors of relationship satisfaction for people with different sexual orientations. The results indicated that the overall model was significant for heterosexual women ($R2 = .61$, $F(3, 209) = 109.24$), $p < .001$) and for lesbians ($R2 = .77$, $F(3, 86) = 97.98$, $p < .001$). In a study of 263 Chinese individuals from Hong Kong living in heterosexual relationships, Ng and Cheng (2010) examined the association of intimacy, passion, and commitment with relationship satisfaction. The results indicated that intimacy and commitment were significantly positively correlated with relationship satisfaction, whereas passion was not.

General Question on the Overall Relationship Quality

A single-item questionnaire on the overall relationship quality developed by the researcher was used to examine the respondents' group membership (positive or negative) with reference to the criterion or dependent variable (relationship quality). The question that was asked is, "How would you rate the overall quality of your relationship with your husband/wife?" The item was answered as either "positive" or "negative." Positive was assigned a value of 1 and negative was assigned a value of 0. Higher scores indicated positive and higher relationship quality.

ANALYSIS

The data analysis for the quantitative phase of the current study included a descriptive statistics analysis, a set of correlation analyses, a multiple linear

regression analysis, and a set of independent-samples t-tests. The researcher used the Statistical Package for Social Sciences (SPSS for Mac, 21.0) for
all these analyses.

Before the analysis was conducted, the researcher defined and labeled
the variables in the SPSS, entered the data, and computed them appropriately. Prior to the computation, the appropriate items on the Relationship
Assessment Scale were reverse scored. The first part of the analyses consisted of describing and summarizing the data by running the descriptive statistics. It included finding the measures of central tendency (mean, median,
and mode) and measures of dispersion (range and standard deviation).

The descriptive statistics analysis looked at the variables in the demographic information schedule, the dependent and independent variables,
the responses in the single item questionnaire on the overall relationship
quality, and the question about interview participation.

The descriptive statistics for the dependent variable of relationship
quality was examined from the Relationship Assessment Scale. The descriptive statistics for the three independent variables of satisfaction, quality of alternatives, and investments were examined from the three subscales
of satisfaction, quality of alternatives, and investments of the Investment
Model Scale respectively. In this analysis, only the global items of the three
subscales of the investment model were used as recommended by the authors, as the facet items were meant only "to enhance the measurement
quality for the global items" (Rusbult et al., 1998, p. 383). The descriptive
statistics for the other three independent variables of intimacy, passion, and
commitment were examined from the three subscales of intimacy, passion,
and commitment of the Triangular Love Scale respectively.

Those variables for which describing the mean was not useful, a frequency distributions analysis was done to describe the number of occurrences and percentages. A frequency distribution analysis was done for the
single item questionnaire about the overall relationship quality as well as
the respondents' willingness to participate in a face-to-face interview.

The descriptive statistics analyses were followed by a set of correlation
bivariate analyses whereby the researcher examined the strength of the association of relationship quality (criterion/dependent variable) with each
of the independent variables (satisfaction, quality of alternatives, investments, intimacy, passion, and commitment).

The bivariate correlation analyses were followed by a multiple linear regression analysis. "Multiple linear regression is a general statistical

procedure for investigating the relation of a single criterion variable to two or more predictor variables" (Sprenkle and Piercy, 2005, p. 383). In the current study, the researcher examined whether the added factors of satisfaction, quality of alternatives, investments, intimacy, passion, and commitment were significantly associated with the relationship quality of the respondents. The analysis measured the strength and direction of association between the dependent and independent variables.

Finally, the data was split by gender, and a series of independent-samples t-tests were run to see whether there was a gender difference with regard to the dependent and independent variables.

9

The Qualitative Phase

STRATEGY: DESCRIPTIVE PHENOMENOLOGY

THE STRATEGY OF INQUIRY that was used for the qualitative phase of the current study is descriptive phenomenology. Phenomenology began in the philosophical reflections of the German mathematician and philosopher, Edmund Husserl during the mid-1890s (Husserl, 1950/1960, 1950/1999). Husserl (1950/1999) defined phenomenology as the "science of pure phenomena" (p. 35). He ushered in a new era of scientific research by inviting investigators to look at things (the phenomena) as they actually appeared, setting aside prejudgments and presuppositions. Thus, a researcher who uses the phenomenological approach begins investigation with "things themselves" or "everyday experience." Such an investigation allows him or her to begin with a state of freshness and openness, free from the customs, beliefs, and prejudices of normal science (Moustakas, 1994). Such an investigation also takes into consideration the importance of the context and settings that provide meaning for the phenomenon (Creswell, 2007; Parra-Cardona et al., 2008).

Seidman (2006) suggested that "people's behavior becomes meaningful and understandable when placed in the context of their lives" (p. 17). Descriptive phenomenology allows the researcher to capture and present a detailed and composite description of the essence and meaning of the participants' lived experiences. In the current study, the researcher stayed true to these characteristics of the phenomenological approach. However, the researcher's role and influence in the study are not to be minimized either. Chawla (2007) noted that in a qualitative study the researcher has multiple roles such as interviewer, observer, and participant, and the researcher's own background has a significant impact on how he or she gathers, understands, and interprets the data. The researcher's role that is discussed above addresses this concern.

PROCEDURE

The subjects were free to choose whether or not to participate in the qualitative phase of the study. Only those who chose to participate in the qualitative interviews were asked to provide their name and contact information, and all others were asked not to write their name or any other identifying information anywhere on the completed questionnaires. Those who volunteered to participate in the qualitative interviews were told that their contact information would be retained for the sole purpose of contacting them again to check the accuracy of their responses (member checking) in the final reports. They were also told that the recordings of qualitative interviews and the transcripts from the qualitative interviews would be kept in a locked, secure cabinet in a locked office that only the researcher had access to.

The interview participants came from a variety of backgrounds with regard to their age, religion, level of education, the duration of marriage, and occupation. In the demographic information table and final reports, pseudonyms are used for the interview participants to protect their confidentiality. Three of the participants (Jaya, Venkatesh, and Srinivas) had consanguineous (uncle-niece) marriages. Although rare, the practice of consanguineous marriage is still found in certain communities in India. One participant (Kavya) came from a matriarchal family. India, in general, is a patriarchal society. However, there are some communities where mother heads the family, and the family descent is determined in the female line. Out of the fourteen subjects, two of them belonged to a couple-dyad, husband and wife. Table 2 contains the demographic information of the participants of the qualitative phase of the study.

Table 2: Demographic Information of the Interview Participants

Participant	Age	Sex	Partner Status	Highest Level of Education	Religion	Nr. Yrs Married	Occupation
Joseph	66	M	Husband	PhD	Catholic	39	Principal
Jaya	66	F	Wife	M.A., B.Ed.	Hindu	49	Teacher
Venkatesh	70	M	Husband	College	Hindu	49	Printing
Priya	32	F	Wife	M.S./IT	Hindu	11	IT
Srinivas	63	M	Husband	MBA	Hindu	30	Teacher
Kavya	32	F	Wife	M. S., M.Ed.	Hindu	10	Teacher
Arpitha	32	F	Wife	M.S./IT	Hindu	12	IT
Renuka	24	F	Wife	M.S., B.Ed.	Hindu	2	Teacher
Peter	28	M	Husband	B.Com	Catholic	2	Banker
Aisha	23	F	Wife	M.A.	Muslim	3	Student
Khadeejah	24	F	Wife	M.A., B.Ed.	Muslim	5	Teacher
Rose	54	F	Wife	M.A., B.Ed.	Catholic	17	Teacher
Thomas	47	M	Husband	M.A., M.Ed.	Catholic	19	Teacher
Mary	36	F	Wife	M.A., B.Ed.	Catholic	10	Teacher

The qualitative phase of the study consisted of one-on-one, face-to-face, open-ended interviews with the participants. To ensure a comfortable and convenient time and place (Speziale and Carpenter, 2007) for the participants, and a hazards-free environment (Easton et al., 2000) for the interviews, the researcher honored the participants' choices with regard to time and location for the interviews.

PHENOMENOLOGICAL INTERVIEW

Roulston et al., (2003) noted that preparing for and doing the interview is not as easy a task as many think. It involves preparing an interview guide and gaining the confidence of the participants. After piloting a preliminary interview guide, the researcher developed a semi-structured interview guide that included nine items with additional questions to enhance the respondents' answers (see Appendix F). The interview guide, modeled on the "Relationship Quality Interview" questionnaire developed by Lawrence et al. (2011), included the particulars of the researcher's introductory conversation with the prospective participants, and questions about their marital relationship. The questions covered areas that were covered in the quantitative phase such as relationship quality, satisfaction, quality of alternatives, investments, intimacy, passion, and commitment. To get a better idea of the respondents' life context and its influence on their marital relationship, questions about the environmental factors influencing their relationship were asked. Examples of questions in the interview guide are, "Now what I would like you to do is, as much as possible, describe in your own words your overall feeling about your marital relationship," and "How would you describe the level of closeness, sense of warmth, affection, and emotional connection you feel with your spouse?"

Successful research, according to Marshall and Rossman (1999) and Speziale and Carpenter (2007) involves mutual trust, cooperation, and respect between the researcher and the participants. Although hospitality is one of the highly valued virtues for Indians in general, when someone approaches them for doing some sort of study, it could be interpreted in many ways, and people could be skeptical about the motives of the researcher. Therefore, with the aim of building rapport and creating a relaxed and trusting atmosphere, the researcher always began the interview process with a brief social conversation (Moustakas, 1994).

Aware that the participants might be at different stages in the continuum of full disclosure and complete secrecy, one of the priorities for the researcher was to respect the participants' autonomy and ensure that they participated in the study voluntarily without being coerced. Hence, before the start of the interview, the researcher thanked the participants for their time and willingness to participate in the study. He told them that there were no right or wrong answers to the questions that he was asking and that he was interested in their particular experiences of being in an arranged marriage and building up a relationship with their spouses. He reminded them that they did not have to answer any question that they were uncomfortable with and that they could stop the interview at any time they wanted.

As mentioned above, the researcher explained to the subjects through the recruitment statement (for survey and interview) and in person (for interviews) the nature, purpose, and requirements of the study that they were undertaking, and sought their verbal consent (Moustakas, 1994; Marshall and Rossman, 1999). Since the subjects who completed the survey had the opportunity to be selected for one-on-one, face-to-face interviews with the researcher, complete anonymity of all the participants was not possible in this study. However, he addressed the confidentiality concerns by ensuring that only the participants and he were in the room at the time of the interview.

He also assured them that no personal information would be shared in the reports or discussions. He was aware that the participants were sharing some of their intimate and personal thoughts in the face-to-face interviews. In the event of any of the participants experiencing any emotional distress as a result of participating in the study, they were free to contact the researcher and adequate arrangements would have been made to refer them for psycho-therapeutic or other mental health services. However, no such issues came up for any of the participants during or after the interviews. The researcher was also aware that it might have been embarrassing for certain participants to discuss their marriage, particularly with a stranger. He addressed this concern by avoiding lengthy and uncomfortable questions.

Using the semi-structured interview guide, the researcher interviewed the subjects, exploring the various dimensions of their marital relationship. Open-ended questions allowed the participants to respond on their own terms and in their own words. However, he was aware that the interview guide was not an instrument meant for a strict structured interview, but rather a tool to assist him to capture the participants' lived experience by engaging in open and exploratory conversations (Speziale and Carpenter, 2007). The researcher often started the interviews with a general conversation about their life and family to create a sense of rapport and comfort for the participants. After getting a sense that the participants were relaxed and comfortable in talking, he focused more on the topic of the study, their marriage and relationship. Occasionally he would ask the participants to elaborate on certain things they mentioned or give him some examples of instances from their marriage or relationship so that he got a better idea of what they were talking about. He used verbal and non-verbal cues to let the participants know that he was following or understanding what they were saying. Each of the interviews lasted approximately an hour.

RECORDING AND TRANSCRIBING

The interview sessions and interactions with the participants were digitally recorded, but the names and identifying information of the participants were excluded from those recordings. Prior to the start of the interview, the participants' permission was sought for digitally recording the interview. After each of the interviews, field notes that combined the researcher's experiences, observations, reactions, and dynamics that occurred during the interviews were prepared. The researcher himself transcribed the recorded data of each of the interviews, and a summary statement of their interviews was sent to the participants to ensure that he had captured their experience and expressions. Some participants, however, said that they trusted the competence of the researcher and did not need any such summary. The field notes and the transcriptions provided broader and deeper understanding of the participants' experiences of their marital relationships.

ANALYSIS

At the completion of the data collection and transcription, an analysis of the qualitative data was done. Roulston et al. (2003) suggested that interviews do not give a pristine and authentic contact with the participants' realities, but rather help the interviewer and the interviewees to co-construct the data that is required for the research project. The researcher felt that the data that he obtained through the interviews were the closest that he could get to about the authentic realities of the participants. An analysis of the data brings order, structure, and interpretation to the massive data collected (Marshall and Rossman, 1999). A six-phased procedure suggested by Marshall and Rossman was used for this data analysis:

Organizing the Data

In a qualitative study, the first task of the researcher after the data collection is to become familiar with the data by reading the transcripts over and over again. This helps to create a picture of each participant's experience as a whole. Some minor editing without losing valuable findings accompanies this process. Accordingly, the researcher read the transcripts over and over again, getting a feel of the data and the experience of each of the participants.

Generating Themes and Patterns

This phase consists of taking note of the salient patterns and themes evident in the setting and participants' expressions. In this process, irrelevant, repetitive, and overlapping data are eliminated. After becoming familiar with the data, the researcher identified specific themes and patterns that stood out in each of the interviews.

Coding the Data

This phase consists of applying some coding scheme to the identified themes and patterns. Codes could take forms such as abbreviation of key words, colored dots, numbers, etc. For example, one of the themes identified from the interviews in the current study was "limited premarital contact." An abbreviation of key words in this theme was coded as "LPC.AM."

Testing Emergent Understanding

As the themes and patterns were being identified and coded, the researcher also evaluated the authenticity of his developing understanding by searching through the data again and determining how useful the data were in illuminating the question(s) being explored.

Searching for Alternative Explanations

As themes and patterns were identified, the researcher critically challenged the very patterns and themes that seemed so apparent. He searched for alternative explanations for these data and then concluded how the already identified explanations were the most authentic of all.

Writing the Report

This is the phase in which the researcher lends shape and form or meaning to the massive amount of raw data. In the current study, this comes under Part IV and Part V, "Research Findings" and "Discussion and Interpretation" respectively.

10

Ethics, Rigor, and Confidentiality

RIGOR AND TRUSTWORTHINESS

To ENSURE RIGOR AND trustworthiness of the findings in a qualitative research, researchers often consider four areas: credibility, dependability, confirmability, and transferability (Shenton, 2004; Speziale and Carpenter, 2007). There are several ways in which researchers establish credibility of the findings such as developing a familiarity with the culture of the participants, writing reflective commentary by the researcher as the project develops, and member checking (Shenton, 2004; Speziale and Carpenter, 2007). Having been born and raised in India, the researcher was quite familiar with the culture and context of the subjects. This familiarity with the culture and context helped him to estimate and minimize the risks to the subjects participating in the study.

As the study progressed, he wrote reflective commentaries from time to time. Member checking is a process of taking the summary or specific descriptions of the interviews back to the interviewees to see whether they considered the summary or descriptions as accurate (Speziale and Carpenter, 2007). In the current study, the participants were given opportunities to read or listen to the summary of the interviews to ensure that the summary had captured their experience and expressions. Some of them, however, declined that suggestion with the comment that they trusted in the competency of the researcher to accurately capture their lived experience.

The dependability issue is addressed by reporting in the text in detail the processes followed in the study so that a future researcher could repeat the work (Shenton, 2004). The detailed description of the processes that was followed in the current study addresses this concern. Confirmability is to ensure that the findings of the study are the result of the experiences and ideas of the participants rather than the opinions and characteristics of the researcher (Shenton, 2004). This is often done by an audit trail, which is a recording of activities during the course of the study so that another individual can trace the course of the research (Shenton, 2004; Speziale and Carpenter, 2007). In the current study, two of the dissertation committee members were asked to function as auditors and go through the audit trail to ensure that there was no mismatch between the participants' views and the researcher's report. However, confirmability, according to Speziale and Carpenter, is a problematic issue in qualitative research. Margarete Sandelowski (as cited in Speziale and Carpenter, 2007) noted that "only the researcher who has collected the data and been immersed in them can confirm the findings" (p. 49).

Transferability, according to Speziale and Carpenter (2007), "refers to the probability that the study findings have meaning to others in similar situations" (p. 49). Researchers differ with regard to the issue of transferability (Shenton, 2004; Speziale and Carpenter, 2007; Sprenkle and Piercy, 2005). Some argue that it is impossible to demonstrate that the findings of a qualitative study are "applicable to other situations and populations" while others reject this notion and argue that findings and conclusions of qualitative projects are transferable (Shenton, 2004, p. 69). In the current study, transferability is not completely ruled out because in spite of the regional differences, there are "some striking generalities" in the family and marital systems across India (Sandhya, 2009, p. 92). These are discussed in Part V under "Discussion and Interpretation."

ETHICAL CONSIDERATIONS

Confidentiality and Consent

As mentioned previously, before conducting the study, the participants were informed about the nature, purpose, and requirements of the current research (Moustakas, 1994; Marshall and Rossman, 1999). They had an opportunity to review the consent form, which was integrated with the recruitment statement. It was mentioned in the consent form that the completion of the survey would indicate their willingness to be subjects in this research. Since the participants who completed the survey had an opportunity to be selected for one-on-one, face-to-face interviews with the researcher, complete anonymity of all the participants was not possible in this study. However, the participants were assured that their identifying information would not be disclosed in any reports or writings.

The participants' permission was sought for the digital recording of the interviews. They were informed of their right to withdraw from the study at any time, for any personal reasons. Even though the identities of the subjects who participated in the qualitative interviews were retained for the purpose of member checking, they were destroyed after it was completed. The surveys, the digital recordings, and the transcriptions of the interviews were kept in a locked, secure cabinet in a locked office that only the researcher had access to. The participants were also assured that all the study data would be destroyed upon the completion of the writing of the final report of the study.

Benefits and Risks for Participants

Regarding benefits, the participants received no direct benefit by participating in this study. However, it was hoped that they might potentially gain some insights into the quality of their own marital relationship. Their participation was expected to benefit others by advancing the research in the field of marriage and family, particularly in reference to arranged marriages in India. Mental health professionals, particularly marital and family therapists, would benefit from this research by learning more about the relationship dynamics in Indian arranged marriages. The study might benefit other couples and families in learning about what others think and feel about arranged marriages.

With regard to the risks involved, the researcher was aware of his task of ensuring the safety and welfare of the participants and protecting them from possible psychological and social harms (Hutchinson et al., 1994; Speziale and Carpenter, 2007). He did not foresee any harm or emotional trauma for the subjects in participating in the present study. However, he was aware that the participants were sharing some of their intimate and personal thoughts with a larger world that was not necessarily intimately connected to them. He was also aware that the interviews might bring back some memories that were very personal, both positive and negative, which they normally might not have shared with anyone else.

In the event of any of the participants experiencing any emotional distress as a result of participating in the study, they were free to contact the researcher and adequate arrangements would have been made to refer them for psychotherapeutic or other mental health services. As hoped, those who participated in the study did not report anything to this effect. The researcher was also aware that it might have been embarrassing for certain participants to discuss about their marriage. He addressed this concern by avoiding the use of lengthy and uncomfortable questions.

PART IV

Research Findings

11

The Quantitative Results

IN LINE WITH THE concurrent triangulation design chosen for the current study, the quantitative and qualitative data were analyzed separately. Since the subjects completed the quantitative measures first and then participated in the qualitative interviews, the analysis was done in that order—that is, the quantitative first and then the qualitative. Although both data sets were given equal priority as suggested for concurrent triangulation designs (Barnes, 2012; Venkatesh et al., 2013), the researcher looked at the qualitative data as a supplement to the quantitative data. The reason for taking that approach was the assumption that the subjects who volunteered and participated in the qualitative interviews were in fact supplementing the quantitative responses they had provided first through the completion of the survey.

Additionally, Creswell (2009) noted, "Ideally, the weight is equal between the two methods, but often in practice, priority may be given to one or the other" (p. 213). Creswell also noted that in most of the published mixed methods studies, researchers present the quantitative results first and then the qualitative results (e.g., Adams-Budde et al., 2014; Boateng, 2009; Massengale et al., 2014). Taking all these into consideration, it was deemed to be a better approach in this study to do the quantitative data analysis first and supplement its results with the results from the qualitative data. This chapter presents the results obtained from the quantitative analysis. A detailed discussion of these results will be done under "Discussion and Interpretation" in Part V.

A total of 287 subjects participated in the quantitative phase of the study, which involved completing a survey. The data analysis for this phase included a set of descriptive statistics analyses, a set of correlation analyses, a multiple linear regression analysis, and a set of independent-samples t-tests. The correlation, regression, and t-test are parametric tests, and one of the assumptions for conducting parametric tests is that the sample is random. The current study used parametric analyses although it used convenience and snowball sampling techniques. This was done after consultation with Dr. Hisako Matsuo, one of the statisticians and research methodology instructors at Saint Louis University. Dr. Matsuo said, "While a random sampling is ideal, it is quite difficult to use the method in reality" (e-mail communication with Dr. Matsuo, November 22, 2013).

DEMOGRAPHIC RESULTS

As the first part of the quantitative analysis, the data was described and summarized by running the descriptive statistics. It included finding the measures of central tendency and measures of dispersion. For those variables for which describing the mean was not useful, a frequency distributions analysis was done to describe the number of occurrences and percentages.

General Question on the Overall Relationship Quality

A frequency distribution analysis was done for the single item questionnaire on the overall relationship quality in this sample. In response, 98.3 percent (282 out of 287) of the subjects rated the overall quality of their marital relationship as positive. Only 1.7 percent (5 out of 287) of the respondents considered the quality of their marital relationship as negative. These results present a very positive and healthy picture of the state of marital relationship in this sample. The results also supported the overall hypothesis of this study that the relationship quality in this sample of the arranged marriages in India is high.

Interview Participation Agreement

A frequency distribution analysis was done for the question regarding the respondents' willingness to participate in the follow-up face-to-face interview. Out of the 287 subjects who completed and returned the questionnaire packets, only forty-eight (17 percent) individuals said "yes" to the follow-up interview. The low response rate could have been because of the participants' fear or nervousness in doing a one-on-one, face-to-face interview with the researcher who is a total stranger to them. Completing a survey was probably much easier and less threatening for many of them than participating in an interview, as the completion of survey ensured complete anonymity.

Those who returned the surveys and volunteered to participate in the interviews were contacted in the order the completed surveys were received. Although forty-eight subjects had volunteered for the interviews, only fourteen were needed to reach the point of saturation, which meant that at the completion of fourteen interviews, the same themes were coming up over and over again and no new information or data was emerging from interviews (Mason, 2010). The fourteen subjects who participated in the interviews were among those who returned the completed questionnaires first.

The participants were informed through the recruitment statement as well as during the distribution of the questionnaires that if they volunteered for the interviews, they would be contacted and interviewed in the order the completed surveys were received. They were also told that if the researcher did not contact them for the interviews their contact information would be destroyed. Accordingly, the contact information of the interview participants were retained for the purpose of member checking, while the contact information of the rest of the volunteers were destroyed.

Dependent and Independent Variables

The research questions that directed this study pertained to the level of satisfaction, quality of alternatives, investments, intimacy, passion, and commitment, and their association with relationship quality in arranged marriages in India. A series of descriptive analyses were performed to obtain the results for the level of each of these variables in the respondents' marital relationships. Table 3 presents the descriptive results of all these variables.

Table 3: Descriptive Statistics of Dependent and Independent Variables

Variable	N	Range	Min.	Max.	Mean	Median	Mode	Std. Deviation
Relationship Quality (DV)	269	27	8	35	29.62	30.00	35	4.687
Satisfaction (IV)	282	40	5	45	38.76	42.00	45	8.265
Alternatives (IV)	272	35	5	40	9.08	5.00	5	6.494
Investment (IV)	279	40	5	45	37.03	40.00	45	8.986
Intimacy (IV)	279	103	32	135	123.65	130.00	135	16.325
Passion (IV)	259	120	15	135	115.20	122.00	135	20.989
Commitment (IV)	267	77	58	135	127.54	133.00	135	12.282

The Relationship Assessment Scale that was used to measure relationship quality is a seven-item, five-point Likert-type scale with scores ranging from 1 (low relationship quality) to 5 (high relationship quality). The total score ranges from 7 (low relationship quality) to 35 (high relationship quality). Higher total scores—that is, scores more than 28—would indicate higher levels of relationship quality and lack of distress in relationships (Hendrick et al., 1998; Renshaw et al., 2010). In the current study, the respondents' total mean score was 29.62, and the median score was 30, both of which according to the RAS represented a high level of relationship quality and lack of distress in their marriage. The results from the RAS are consistent with the results of the single item questionnaire on the subjects' overall assessment of their marital relationship. Ninety-eight percent of the subjects had responded that their marital relationship was positive.

The Investment Model Scale (IMS) that was used to examine the respondents' level of satisfaction, quality of alternatives, and investments is a nine-point Likert-type scale with scores ranging from 1 (do not agree at all) to 9 (agree completely).

The total score of the satisfaction scale of the IMS ranges from 5 to 45, and higher scores on the scale represent a higher satisfaction and lower scores represent lower satisfaction (Etcheverry et al., 2013; Macher, 2013; Rusbult et al., 1998). The subjects in the current study obtained a total mean of 38.76 and a median of 42 for satisfaction. Both these scores according to the standards of the scale represented a healthy and strong level of satisfaction in the subjects' marital relationship (Rusbult et al., 1998; Vanderdrift et al., 2012).

Given that the total score of the quality of alternatives scale in the IMS ranges from 5 to 45, the subjects in the current study obtained a total mean of 9.08, and median score of 5 for their quality of alternatives. Both these scores being very low, the study indicated that the level of quality of alternatives in this sample was weak, which in turn meant that their marriages were high quality relationships (Rodrigues and Lopes, 2013; Rusbult et al., 1998).

The total score of the investments scale of the IMS ranged from 5 to 45, and higher scores on the scale represent a higher investment size and lower scores on the scale represent lower investment size (Macher, 2013; Vanderdrift et al., 2012; Rusbult et al., 1998). The subjects in the current study obtained a total mean of 37.03 and a median of 40 for investments. According to the standards of the IMS, both the mean and median obtained in this study are high scores, which means that in this sample, the subjects have made a great deal of investments into their marital relationships.

The Triangular Love Scale (TLS), which is a nine-point Likert-type scale with scores ranging from 1 (not at all), to 9 (extremely) was used to examine the respondents' level of intimacy, passion, and commitment.

The total score for the intimacy scale in the TLS ranges from 15 (low intimacy) to 135 (high intimacy). In the current study, the respondents' total mean score for intimacy was 123.65, and the median score was 130. Both the mean and the median according to the standards of the TLS indicate that the subjects in the current study have a strong and healthy level of intimacy in their marriage (Overbreek et al., 2007; Panayiotou, 2005; Sternberg, 1986). In other words, the results suggest that for the subjects and their partners there is a mutual feeling of closeness, connectedness, and affection in their spousal relationship (Heller and Wood, 2000; Moore et al., 2001; Sternberg, 1986).

The total score for the passion scale in the TLS ranges from 15 (low passion) to 135 (high passion). The subjects obtained a total mean score of 115.20, and a median score of 122 for the variable of passion. Both these scores, the mean and the median, were high scores according to the standards of the scale. These results thus indicate that the subjects in this sample have a strong sense of passion in their marriages (Panayiotou, 2005; Sternberg, 1986).

The total score for the commitment scale in the TLS ranges from 15 (low commitment) to 135 (high commitment). The total mean score of the respondents' commitment was 127.54, and they had a median score of 133. Both the mean and the median according to the standards of the scale represented high commitment in the subjects' marriages (Overbreek et al., 2007; Panayiotou, 2005; Sternberg, 1986). It means that the subjects in this study have a strong sense of commitment in their marriages. In other words, their sense of allegiance and love toward each other and their intent to maintain and persist in that love relationship are strong (Rusbult et al., 1998; Sternberg, 1986).

BIVARIATE CORRELATION ANALYSES

The first set of the research hypotheses in the present study pertained to the strength of association between relationship quality and each of the independent variables: satisfaction, quality of alternatives, investments, intimacy, passion, and commitment. A series of bivariate correlation analyses were conducted to test these associations. As mentioned before, the Relationship Assessment Scale measured the dependent variable of relationship quality, and the respective subscales of the Investment Model Scale and the Triangular Love Scale measured the independent variables of satisfaction, alternatives, investments, intimacy, passion, and commitment. In the following sections, each of the research hypotheses will be restated and the pertinent results obtained from the correlation analyses will be reported.

Hypothesis 1: The respondents' marital satisfaction shows a significant positive correlation with their relationship quality.

The results obtained from the correlation analysis supported the hypothesis that a statistically significant positive correlation between satisfaction and relationship quality in this sample exists ($r = .69$, $p < .001$). It means that for this sample, satisfaction in marriage is positively associated with their relationship quality. The descriptive statistical results presented above showed that this sample had a high satisfaction rate, and the correlation results confirmed a significant association between the subjects' marital satisfaction and their relationship quality.

Hypothesis 2: The respondents' quality of alternatives shows a significant negative correlation with their relationship quality.

The results obtained from the correlation analysis confirmed the hypothesis that a statistically significant negative correlation between the respondents' quality of alternatives and their relationship quality exists ($r = -.21$, $p = .001$). It means that for this sample of the arranged marriages in

India, the quality of alternatives is an influencing factor in their relationship quality. The subjects perceive that their current marital relationship is the best that they could have had to fulfill their most important needs. They would not trade their partners for anyone else. The alternative relationships that could fulfill their most important needs are thus presumably low or weak. The correlation results thus confirmed a significant association between the quality of alternatives and relationship quality in this sample.

Hypothesis 3: The investment of resources in the respondents' marriage shows a significant positive correlation with their relationship quality.

The current study explored whether there was an association between the investment size and relationship quality in this sample of the arranged marriages in India. The results obtained from the correlation analysis confirmed the hypothesis that a statistically significant positive correlation between the respondents' investments and relationship quality exists ($r = .38$, $p < .001$). It means that for this sample of the arranged marriages in India, the investment of resources is a positive influencing factor in their relationship quality. The more they invest into their marital relationship, the greater will be their relationship quality. The descriptive statistical results presented above showed that this sample had a healthy level of investments, and the correlation results confirmed a significant association between the respondents' investment size and their relationship quality.

Hypothesis 4: Intimacy in the respondents' marital relationship shows a significant positive correlation with their relationship quality.

The results obtained from the correlation analysis confirmed the hypothesis that a statistically significant positive correlation between the respondents' level of intimacy and relationship quality exists ($r = .71$, $p < .001$). It means that for this sample, intimacy has a positive influence on their relationship quality. It also means that for this sample, as the level of their intimacy in marriage increases the level of their relationship quality also increases. The descriptive statistical results presented above showed that this sample had a very healthy and strong level of intimacy, and the correlation results confirmed a significant association between the two variables of intimacy and relationship quality in this sample.

Hypothesis 5: Passion in the respondents' marital relationship shows a significant positive correlation with their relationship quality.

The results obtained from the correlation analysis supported the hypothesis that a statistically significant positive correlation between the respondents' level of passion and relationship quality exists ($r = .60$, $p < .001$).

It means that for this sample of the arranged marriages in India, the variable of passion has a positive influence on their relationship quality. It also means that for this sample, as the level of passion in marriage increases the level of their relationship quality also increases. The descriptive statistical results presented above showed that this sample had a high level of passion, and the correlation results confirmed a significant association between the respondents' passion and their relationship quality.

Hypothesis 6: Commitment in the respondents' marital relationship shows a significant positive correlation with their relationship quality.

The results of this study confirmed the hypothesis that a statistically significant positive correlation between the respondents' level of commitment and relationship quality exists ($r = .57, p < .001$). It means that for this sample of the arranged marriages in India, commitment in marriage has a positive influence on their relationship quality. It also means that for this sample, as the level of their commitment in marriage increases the level of their relationship quality also increases. The descriptive statistical results presented above showed that this sample had a strong and healthy level of marital commitment, and the correlation results confirmed a significant association between the two variables of marital commitment and relationship quality in this sample.

Table 4 presents the inter-correlations among all the variables. The correlations between all the independent variables were generally moderate.

Table 4: Correlations Matrix

		Rel.Q.	Sat.	Alt.	Inv.	Int.	Pas.	Com.
Rel. Quality	Pearson Correlation	1	.690**	-.207**	.384**	.708**	.594**	.568**
	Sig. (2-tailed)		.000	.001	.000	.000	.000	.000
Satisfaction	Pearson Correlation	.690**	1	-.325**	.425**	.755**	.639**	.596**
	Sig. (2-tailed)	.000		.000	.000	.000	.000	.000
Alternatives	Pearson Correlation	-.207**	-.325**	1	-.220**	-.304**	-.358**	-.351**
	Sig. (2-tailed)	.001	.000		.000	.000	.000	.000
Investment	Pearson Correlation	.384**	.425**	-.220**	1	.603**	.541**	.520**
	Sig. (2-tailed)	.000	.000	.000		.000	.000	.000
Intimacy	Pearson Correlation	.708**	.755**	-.304**	.603**	1	.768**	.800**
	Sig. (2-tailed)	.000	.000	.000	.000		.000	.000
Passion	Pearson Correlation	.594**	.639**	-.358**	.541**	.768**	1	.704**
	Sig. (2-tailed)	.000	.000	.000	.000	.000		.000
Commitment	Pearson Correlation	.568**	.596**	-.351**	.520**	.800**	.704**	1
	Sig. (2-tailed)	.000	.000	.000	.000	.000	.000	

**. Correlation is significant at the 0.01 level (2-tailed).

MULTIPLE LINEAR REGRESSION ANALYSIS

Hypothesis 7: The added factors of marital satisfaction, quality of alternatives, investments, intimacy, passion, and commitment in the respondents' marriage show a significant relationship with their relationship quality.

A multiple linear regression analysis was conducted to examine whether the added factors of satisfaction, quality of alternatives, investments, intimacy, passion, and commitment were significantly associated with the relationship quality of the respondents. The multiple linear regression analysis measured the strength and direction of the association between the dependent variable and the combined independent variables. Table 5 presents the results of this analysis.

Table 5: Multiple Linear Regression

Model Summary				
Model	R	R Square	Adjusted R Square	Std. Error of the Estimate
1	.774a	.599	.588	3.084

a. Predictors: (Constant), Commitment, Quality of Alternatives, Investment, Satisfaction, Passion, Intimacy

ANOVA[a]						
Model		Sum of Squares	df	Mean Square	F	Sig.
1	Regression	3032.068	6	505.345	53.131	.000[b]
	Residual	2025.910	213	9.511		
	Total	5057.977	219			

a. Dependent Variable: RAS

b. Predictors: (Constant), Commitment, Quality of Alternatives, Investment, Satisfaction, Passion, Intimacy

Coefficients[a]					
Model	Unstandardized Coefficients		Standardized Coefficients	t	Sig.
	B	Std. Error	Beta		
(Constant)	4.793	2.450		1.957	.052
Satisfaction	.178	.042	.309	4.247	.000
Quality of Alternatives	.040	.034	.056	1.186	.237
1 Investment	.009	.031	.016	.292	.770
Intimacy	.150	.029	.517	5.183	.000
Passion	.009	.017	.041	.554	.580
Commitment	-.018	.029	-.046	-.616	.538
a. Dependent Variable: RAS					

The analysis found a significant linear regression equation that produced $F(6, 213) = 53.131$, $p < .001$, with an R^2 of .599 (see Table 5).

The Model Summary section in Table 5 contains the R Square value (.599), which explains the variability in the dependent variable by the combined influence of the independent variables. It means that in the current study, 59.9 percent of the variance in relationship quality was explained by the combined influence of the independent variables. In other words, all of the variables together—satisfaction, quality of alternatives, investments, intimacy, passion, and commitment—represent about 60 percent of the factors that contribute to the relationship quality in this sample of the arranged marriages in India, leaving 40 percent of the relationship quality unexplained or not accounted for by these variables. This is a relatively high R Square value, since the rule of thumb is to have at least 30 percent of the variance explained by the statistical model to consider it as significant.

The analysis of variance (ANOVA) calculated on this regression equation was significant ($F(6, 213) = 53.131$, $p < .001$; see Table 5), demonstrating that the added factors of marital satisfaction, quality of alternatives, investment of resources, intimacy, passion, and commitment contribute significantly to the relationship quality in this sample. Based on these results, the research hypothesis about the added factors of satisfaction, alternatives, investments, intimacy, passion, and commitment in the respondents' marriage showing a significant positive relationship with their relationship quality is confirmed.

The table of coefficients in the third section of Table 5 shows the relationship between the independent variables and the dependent variable. Notably the statistical significance of the multiple linear regression is found only when all the independent variables are combined. Although each of the independent variables showed statistically significant relationship with the dependent variable in the bivariate correlation analyses, they didn't show the same results in the regression analysis because the significance of the multiple linear regression is obtained only when it looks at the combined effect of all the independent variables on the dependent variable rather than looking at their effects separately. Taken separately, as shown in the coefficients table, each of them does not show a significant relationship with relationship quality in the regression analysis. The t-statistics and the p-values in the table show that taken separately, the quality of alternatives ($t = 1.19, p = .24$), investments ($t = .29, p = .77$), passion ($t = .55, p = .58$), and commitment ($t = -.62, p = .54$) do not seem to be contributing to the relationship quality. Only satisfaction ($t = 4.25, p < .001$) and intimacy ($t = 5.18, p < .001$) show a statistically significant relationship. Therefore, it is to be noted that for this sample, the multiple linear regression is significant only when the variables are in combination with each other rather than on their own.

INDEPENDENT-SAMPLES T-TESTS: GENDER DIFFERENCE

Hypothesis 8: There is a significant difference between men and women in their assessment of relationship quality, satisfaction, quality of alternatives, investments, intimacy, passion, and commitment.

One of the research questions was whether there was a difference between men and women in arranged marriages in India in their assessment of satisfaction, quality of alternatives, investments, intimacy, passion, commitment, and the overall relationship quality. Studies done on marriages of choice and romantic relationships, such as those done by Rusbult et al. (1998) and Rhyne (1981), had shown that men and women had differed in their assessment of some of these variables.

To see whether there was a significant gender difference with regard to the dependent and independent variables in the current study, the data was split by gender, and a series of independent-samples t-tests were calculated comparing the mean scores of men to the mean scores of women. There was one couple-dyad in the subset of the sample that participated in the interviews. Otherwise, both males and females in this sample were assumed to be independent of each other. The t-tests were also based on the assumption of the equality of variances. Levene's test for equality of variances showed that except for satisfaction, the variances were equal or the distribution of scores of each of the variables was similar in shape. No significant difference was found between the two groups for any of the variables. Hence the research hypothesis on gender difference with regard to each of the variables remained unconfirmed. Table 6 presents the results of this analysis.

Table 6: Independent-Samples t-tests

	Gender	Mean	Std. Deviation	Sig. (2-tailed)
Relationship Quality	Male	30.45	4.379	.105
	Female	29.37	4.760	
Satisfaction	Male	40.12	6.777	.084
	Female	38.35	8.641	
Quality of Alternatives	Male	9.29	6.757	.776
	Female	9.02	6.428	
Investments	Male	37.25	9.146	.827
	Female	36.97	8.957	
Intimacy	Male	123.74	16.311	.959
	Female	123.62	16.367	
Passion	Male	115.68	20.581	.836
	Female	115.05	21.169	
Commitment	Male	126.77	13.607	.578
	Female	127.77	11.878	

Note: **For all variables, $p > .05$**

The result indicated that for this sample of the arranged marriages in India, no significant difference between men and women in their assessment of relationship quality existed ($t(267) = 1.625$, $p > .05$). The mean scores of the males ($M = 30.45$, $SD = 4.379$) are slightly higher than the mean of the females ($M = 29.37$, $SD = 4.760$), but the scores between the groups are not significantly different (see Table 6).

The results show no significant difference between men and women in their satisfaction level ($t(135.513) = 1.738, p > .05$). The mean scores for males ($M = 40.12$, $SD = 6.777$) are slightly higher than the mean scores for females ($M = 38.35$, $SD = 8.641$). Their standard deviations are also slightly different. However, the scores between the groups are not significantly different ($p = .084$; see Table 6).

The study indicates that for this sample of the arranged marriages in India, no significant difference between men and women in their assessment of quality of alternatives exists ($t(270) = .285$, $p > .05$). The mean scores for males ($M = 9.29$, $SD = 6.757$) are slightly higher than the mean for females ($M = 9.02$, $SD = 6.428$). Their standard deviations are about the same. However, the mean scores between the groups are not significantly different ($p = .776$). Both groups seem to be suggesting that their current relationship is the best to fulfill their most important needs (see Table 6).

The results show no significant difference between men and women concerning the investment of resources ($t(277) = .219$; $p > .05$). Although the mean score for males ($M = 37.25$, $SD = 9.146$) is slightly higher than the mean for females ($M = 36.97$, $SD = 8.957$), the scores between the groups are not significantly different ($p = .827$; see Table 6).

The study indicates that for this sample, no significant difference between men and women in their assessment of intimacy exists ($t(277) = .051$, $p > .05$). Although the mean score for males ($M = 123.74$, $SD = 16.311$) is slightly higher than the mean for females ($M = 123.62$, $SD = 16.367$), and their standard deviations are about the same, there is no significant difference between the groups in their scores (see Table 6).

The results in this study show that no statistically significant difference between men and women in their level of passion exists ($t(257) = .207$, $p > .05$). Although the mean score for males ($M = 115.68$, $SD = 20.581$) is slightly higher than the mean for females ($M = 115.05$, $SD = 21.169$), the scores are not significantly different ($p = .836$; see Table 6).

The results show that in this sample of the arranged marriages in India, no significant difference between men and women in their assessment of commitment exists ($t(265) = -.556$, $p > .05$). The mean score for males ($M = 126.77$, $SD = 13.607$) is slightly lower than the mean for females ($M = 127.77$, $SD = 11.878$). However, the scores between the groups are not significantly different ($p = .578$; see Table 6).

All the independent-samples t-tests thus show no significant difference between men and women in this sample in the assessment of any of the variables.

12

The Qualitative Results

THE ANALYSIS OF THE quantitative data was followed by an analysis of the qualitative data. The fourteen individuals, Joseph, Jaya, Venkatesh, Priya, Srinivas, Kavya, Arpitha, Renuka, Peter, Aisha, Khadeejah, Rose, Thomas, and Mary who participated in the qualitative interviews shared their experiences about their marriage and relationship with their spouses. As mentioned, the names used for the interview participants in this report are pseudonyms to protect the confidentiality of the subjects.

A six-phased procedure suggested by Marshall and Rossman (1999) was used for the analysis of the data collected. The six phases of the procedure were: organizing the data, generating themes and patterns, coding the data, testing emergent understanding, searching for alternative explanations, and writing the report. An analysis of the experiences reported by the participants revealed five major themes and their sub-themes. To substantiate the accuracy of the themes and findings, quotes and comments from the interviewees are referenced in this report with line numbers of interview transcripts given in parenthesis. Table 7 presents an outline of all these themes and sub-themes.

Table 7: Outline of Themes from the Qualitative Data

Theme 1: Family Involvement

    Sub-theme 1: Family Involvement in Partner Choices

    Sub-theme 2: Consulting Children in Partner Choices

    Sub-theme 3: Family Involvement After Marriage

Theme 2: Limited Premarital Contact

Theme 3: Essential Elements for Success

    Sub-theme 1: Acceptance and Understanding

    Sub-theme 2: Adjustment and Compromise

    Sub-theme 3: Shared Values and Responsibilities

    Sub-theme 4: Little Instances of Love

    Sub-theme 5: Religion and Spirituality

Theme 4: Assessment of Marital Relationship

    Sub-theme 1: Satisfaction

    Sub-theme 2: Quality of Alternatives

    Sub-theme 3: Investment of Resources

    Sub-theme 4: Intimacy

    Sub-theme 5: Passion

    Sub-theme 6: Commitment

Theme 5: Persistence in Marriage as a Priority

THEME 1: FAMILY INVOLVEMENT

One of the major themes that emerged from the phenomenological interviews was family involvement. The participants shared that family's involvement in arranged marriages in India is a given. It is an unwritten expectation of both parents and children. Children hope that the parents or the responsible adults in the family would take the initiative in getting their marriages arranged. They also expect the families to meet the expenses associated with their wedding, help them to settle down after the wedding, and continue to support them in as many ways as possible in the subsequent years.

Parents or the families consider it their duty, right, and privilege to do the same. The participants reiterated that that is how the collectivistic culture in India functions, and several of them gave the impression that it was the right way to do it. They found the family involvement as a good thing rather than something negative. Many of the subjects were grateful that their parents or family members were involved in their marital decision-making process and thereafter. Some of the specific ways in which the family becomes an active participant in these arranged marriages are explained under the following sub-themes: family involvement in partner choices, consulting children in partner choices, and parents' involvement after marriage.

Sub-theme 1: Family Involvement in Partner Choices

All the participants said that their families were actively involved in picking their partners. The majority of them believed that their parents were wiser in recognizing and choosing the best match for them. One of the subjects, Rose, for example, was very convinced that her parents knew who would be the best match for her. She stated, "I always think that my father will make the right choice. . . . I said, if he takes a decision, it will be only for my good" (Rose, 53–54). Another subject, Thomas, said something very similar to this, "Yes, I am very happy and they [his parents] took the right decision" (Thomas, 13). Venkatesh, who had a consanguineous (uncle-niece) marriage, shared how he found his spouse, "My co-brother [half-brother] suggested to me this relationship" (Venkatesh, 17). Another participant, Priya, described how her family went about with the arrangement of her marriage:

> I come from a very conservative Brahmin [Hindu] family. Actually, when we plan to get married and all that, it is actually our parents who take the responsibility of the marriage. So as a result, my name, my bio data, and all that was registered with marriage bureau. . . . Similarly, even my husband's parents, they had taken the initiative and they had registered his name and his bio data, and we continue this marriage proposal, everything based on horoscope [a practice among certain Hindus]. First our horoscopes had to be matched, and we saw that out of the total number of those matching, they take a lot of things into consideration. Out of thirty-six, ours matched up to thirty-three, and that was the basis. So, we people, my parents called their parents and an interview was set up. Like this we had shortlisted almost three, four guys. . . . When we had this interview, during the first interview itself, though we did not speak personally and all those things, first time itself it

was okay and it went to the next stage and consecutively after two, three meetings, our marriage was fixed. (Priya, 3–16)

One subject, Aisha, gave the full credit to her parents for choosing the right man for her. She stated, "My parents arranged this marriage. I gave my consent. I consented them. I loved the man, and so I consented" (Aisha, 3–4). Another subject, Srinivas, reiterated the same, "Everyone was involved" (Srinivas, 42).

One subject, Peter, said that his parents took the initiative in finding a girl and getting him married, although he himself was not thinking about marriage at that time. But that didn't mean that they forced him to get married. He stated:

> When I was working for a bank, my parents wanted me to get married, because I was all alone in Hyderabad, outside (a city away from home). Then I thought, I was not interested actually that time, because I wanted to be a priest initially when I completed my B.Com. I joined even one seminary, and then even my brother was and both sisters were in congregations (religious orders). So, they [parents] told me, [to] get married. Then I told, Ok. Then they searched [for] one girl . . . first time I saw her, then I told let us decide. Then I went back again. Then we spoke in phone, we have telephone communication and all. Then we decided okay, let us decide. Then again, we came back; I came back for holidays. Then we had discussion all that, when I can get married. Then the date got fixed. (Peter, 3–12)

These responses from the subjects and the overall results from the qualitative interviews indicated that the families of the respondents actively participated in arranging their marriages. Seemingly most participants were happy about the involvement of their families and felt encouraged by it.

Sub-theme 2: Consulting Children in Partner Choices

The participants felt that it was important to communicate about their role in choosing their partners as well. They said that arranging a marriage in India was a lengthy process. Parents were not just choosing somebody and forcing their decision upon the children. They were consulted in picking their partners. None of them was forced into marriage or forced to choose their partners. They had the freedom to accept or reject the partners their parents had identified for them. If they didn't like one, they could look for another proposal. One of the subjects, Jaya, was very clear about this freedom when she said, "Yea, I can refuse. If I don't like, I don't marry him" (Jaya, 69). Renuka, another subject, also was very specific about her freedom to choose her partner when she said, "No. No force" (Renuka, 29). Arpitha, another participant, said that her parents wanted her to get married, but they did not force her, "They didn't put any pressure on me" (Arpitha, 8).

One respondent, Joseph, shared that his father was a highly educated man and he respected his freedom with regard to his education, career, and marriage. Talking about the conversation that he had with his father before choosing his partner, he reported:

> In the year 1971, I started working. Then when I completed two years of service, my father asked me, don't you feel alone in Karnataka (one of the states in India). Don't you need a partner? You choose one for yourself or I will help you in choosing the partner. And then he gave me freedom, freedom to choose, but he also said, I can help you if you want. I kept quiet, and then said, oh no, dad, you can just go ahead if you have somebody in your mind or why don't you give some help. And so, it happened that, one day I was doing my valuation work, and [dad] just called me up and said, one of our relatives has just suggested a name, are you interested? She is from a particular part of Kerala, and distantly related to us. (Joseph, 4–12)

The participants' responses indicate that they were not forced into marriage or accepting their marital partners but rather were involved in the decision-making processes.

Sub-theme 3: Family Involvement After Marriage

Some participants shared that their parents continued to involve themselves and influenced their day-to-day affairs even after their marriage. Some of them liked it while others gave the impression that they could have done without it. One participant, Rose, found the involvement of her family after her marriage very helpful. She stated, "Yeah, my brother-in-law is not married. My husband's brother, he is not interested in getting married. He gives us support. Financially also. And financially and other ways. My sisters-in-law also are very nice people. Even, even they came, when I was bed-ridden, even they came forward and they used to help my husband in all his work" (Rose, 154–57).

Thomas, another participant, stated that he was the primary caregiver for his aged parents. His parents and the extended family continued to be part of his life even after marriage. He stated, "When I left the parents, I found it very difficult, to be here, in this place. My place here was too hard. And for a week, again, we had to go to my parents, morning and evening. So, she [wife] also came with me, that time, accompanied me. So, really, I felt very bad to leave my parents. Even now also I go thrice in a week to meet my parents. She also comes with me. . . . Only my parents are there. They are aged" (Thomas, 172–78).

Arpitha reported that her parents and in-laws were actively involved in their life. She said:

> She [mother-in-law] doesn't want me to come and stay with her also leaving her son. She feels that I have to comfort her son even if I don't come and take care of her or be there. Usually I have seen a few families where mother-in-law insists on coming and staying there for months together to do some work, to learn the work immediately after marriage. But she says, "I want my son to be happy." That's the support that she has given. And any time, any small inconveniences I have with health or other issues, my parents immediately come and stay with me. That support completely I have, parents, mother, and my brother-in-law is a psychiatrist. He is here, and he is very helpful. (Arpitha, 144–52)

Some participants indicated that they didn't have much choice about the involvement of their parents either because they lived with their parents after marriage or because their spouses allowed their parents to get involved in their day-to-day affairs and decision-making processes. In some families, children stay with their parents even after their marriage. In such cases, the father/father-in-law is the major decision maker in the family. Aisha, one of the interview participants, indicated that she had such a family, and she did not seem to be very happy about the decision-making process in her family. "My husband's father makes all the decisions. . . . But it is very difficult to follow. . . . We follow the decision from my husband's father" (Aisha, 161, 172–73).

The results thus show that family involvement is a constant feature in the life of the subjects before and after their marriage. The majority of the subjects reported that they appreciated the involvement of the family, while some appeared to resent it.

THEME 2: LIMITED PREMARITAL CONTACT

One of the major themes that stood out in all the interviews was the limited premarital contact. The subjects had limited knowledge about their spouses before their marriage. The participants reported that even though they met their prospective spouses once or twice prior to their marriage, the meetings were often in the presence of other family members, and the conversations were very brief. Thomas, one of the subjects, illustrated this point when he said:

> I did not know anything about her. Then after the proposal, I had the opportunity to meet her—that is, I went to their house to know something in detail two, three times. Then I was so much impressed by her parents and her brothers and sisters, everybody. Short visit and conversations with her. After engagement, not before, one or two weeks, that means, after our engagement, engagement only, not before. After engagement. No hours. It was five minutes or ten minutes. That's all. Yeah. Then I came to know more about their family. Yeah. Arranged marriage is like that (laughs). It is a meeting between two strangers, ah, it was not difficult for me. . . . I am very, very happy with the arranged marriage. Nobody forced. (Thomas, 16–41)

When the researcher asked Renuka, another subject, whether she had a chance to meet or talk to her spouse before marriage, she said, "No, no. Only after arranging it, we met" (Renuka, 24). Rose, one of the participants, said that she had no knowledge of the whereabouts of her husband before marriage. She said, "I didn't know anything about him" (Rose, 51). Jaya, another participant, shared that her interaction with her husband before their marriage consisted of just one letter from him. She reported, "I think, before marriage, he wrote a letter, I think, about, just general. Letter said something like we can live happily, I hope you can understand me, I will also cooperate, something like that. So, he wrote a letter like that. I didn't reply" (Jaya, 80–85).

Mary, one of the subjects, reported that she and her husband had very limited knowledge of each other before their marriage. She said, "I did not know him. Not much. Like strangers" (Mary, 68). Aisha, another subject, said that she met her husband just once before marriage. She stated, "In our community, it [meeting or extensive interaction before marriage] is not allowed. Because, eh, we are not familiar. And, ah, he is an unknown person to me. So, they did not allow me to phone to him. And once I met him before marriage . . . we spoke for two hours" (Aisha, 27–36).

Renuka, one of the participants, stated that although she and her husband were like strangers when they came into their marriage, it did not take much time for them to bond and become intimate. She reported, "Actually for us it was not that difficult, because somehow we both are [have] same behavior and same type of likings" (Renuka, 40–41). Peter, another participant, shared that he had very limited interaction with his wife before marriage. "We used to have talk in phone, then once or twice I met [her] before marriage" (Peter, 32–33).

All the subjects thus shared about the limited knowledge and interactions they had about and with their marital partners before their marriages. Except one subject, no one else seemed to be too much bothered about such unwritten rules regarding interactions between men and women before marriage. This theme of limited knowledge and interactions before marriage is reflected in the title of this study, *Strangers to Spouses*.

THEME 3: ESSENTIAL ELEMENTS FOR SUCCESS

All of the participants, except one, said that overall, they were very happy about their marriage, and considered the relationship with their spouses as positive. They listed a few things as essential elements responsible for the success in their marriages. They are: acceptance and understanding, adjustment and compromise, shared values and responsibilities, little instances of love, and religion and spirituality.

Sub-theme 1: Acceptance and Understanding

The majority of the participants spoke repeatedly about acceptance and understanding as very important elements for the success in their marriage. Joseph, one of the subjects, talked about what he meant by acceptance: "Acceptance. I have accepted her totally. She has accepted me totally with all my weaknesses. . . . We had good understanding. Never, never I had to ask her for anything. She would understand my needs and make sure that I get it. We complement each other. I am so lucky" (Joseph, 194–96, 206).

Arpitha, one of the participants, said that in an arranged marriage, it was important for partners to give each other some time, so that they can understand each other. She stated, "Try to understand your husband or partner, and then you give them their space to settle down with you" (Arpitha, 98–99). Jaya, another participant, shared about how she supported and accepted her husband, especially when he was going through a difficult time emotionally and financially. "There is so much of understanding and gave support, I supported him like anything. He should not in anyway get that frustration" (Jaya, 179–80).

Priya, one of the subjects, described how her husband was very understanding and accepting even when she made mistakes. She said, "First of all, I think it is my husband's character. Some good, he is actually a very good, down-to-earth fellow, and I don't have any inhibitions with him. And he is very supportive even though, ah, what I feel. Even though I made few mistakes he took it very sportively, maybe, and the trust I have in him helped me a lot. Yes. He is, he has got too much patience" (Priya, 64–69).

Sub-theme 2: Adjustment and Compromise

Several of the participants shared that a lot of adjustments and compromises were needed to keep their marriage strong and happy. Jaya, one subject, expressed her views on this theme. "Understanding each and sacrificing, compromises, accepting the things [are] important for a happy marriage" (Jaya, 226–27). Kavya, another participant, when referring to adjustments and compromises in her marriage, stated:

> In the beginning I told you, I have a satisfied family life, I would say. But when I say satisfied, I would say, it means that it has a lot of compromises and adjustments. Because we are all, we come from two different backgrounds. We were strangers. We have different tastes. So when two people like that come together, there will be, we have to make a lot of compromises. So a lot of compromise and adjustment make our family strong. So even just a few hours before also I had a fight with him. . . . I had taken an appointment for the dentist. . . . He is fond of sleeping. So, he would say, I have not slept until now. So, he would ask me to take my son to the dentist. I want to sleep, he would say. . . . Why do you make a fuss about it, I asked. Then he said, you are always like that. You would not try to understand me or my situation. (Kavya, 531–43)

Renuka, one of the respondents, considered adjustment as one of the essential elements of successful marriage. She shared about what she meant by adjustments. "Adjustment means care and love, knowing each other, helping each other. . . . Behavior-wise, yes. Background, to some extent, but mostly behavior" (Renuka, 50–53). Peter, another respondent, talked about the little things in their everyday life where they had to make a lot of adjustments:

> Yes. We have to adjust with each other. Because, when she likes some food, I have to eat that. So I tell, cook fish today, then she will tell, no, I don't want to eat fish today. Then [I would say] okay, fine, like that. And sometimes, she wants to go home, then I will not be having holidays, so I will tell, no. Then she will have one relative's marriage, so she wants to go. Then I will tell no, let us not go this time, like that. So, she adjusts. Yeah (laughs), we have to do that in a married life. Sometimes I feel, oh why I got married, sometimes, sometimes, just for one hour or half an hour like that, just like that. Oh, I would have been happy if I was a bachelor, I could have gone anywhere. (Peter, 124–28)

Another subject, Khadeejah, shared similar feelings about adjustments in family life. "We have to adjust with the situations. Mainly, both of them, both men and women, have to adjust with the situations. If men have some work or like that, the women have to adjust with that situation, and cooperate with him" (Khadeejah, 95–97). Priya, one of the participants, reported that she felt very comfortable with her husband. She didn't have to pretend or do things to make him happy. He accepted and loved her as she was. She said, "For me, one thing is, I am actually myself with my husband. I don't have any, I am my true self with my husband. So that's it. I don't need to pretend, or I need not be anybody else. I can be my true self with my husband. So obviously I am always intimate with him" (Priya, 160–66).

Sub-theme 3: Shared Values and Responsibilities

The participants talked about the importance of having shared values and responsibilities in making their marriages successful. One subject, Priya, sounded very positive about her husband and described how he helped her with the household chores and other tasks. She even compared him to other husbands and said that he was the best. She said:

> Yeah, yeah, he does a lot and helps unlike many husbands in India. He takes care of my daughter, when I am not available. He helps with groceries, shopping, all those things. Even at home, suppose he is reading a book he would come out with the gist of the book when we take coffee in the morning when everybody is asleep,

we would get up early, share some half an hour, like that. So even actually he is very busy with his office and but still he takes some time to see that, as soon I come home, he would ask "how was your day, how were your friends, what did you do in the college," and all that. The same thing with my daughter also. We spend some time and he helps me a lot, when guests are there he would help with the kitchen, cooking and all that. (Priya, 123–31)

Renuka, one of the subjects, shared that her husband consulted her before making any decision, and he helped her with household chores. This is what she said: "Yeah, he consults. For each and everything he consults. . . . Yeah, everything, household work, cleaning, and everything . . . daily he will help me" (Renuka, 138). Joseph, another subject, said that in addition to sharing the household tasks and responsibilities, he and his wife shared many values and principles in common, and that made their life and relationship stronger. He stated:

We always believe in sharing; sharing in the sense, you know, at home we share, the household chores we share, about taking care of children, we shared. There was no complaint. We had good understanding. . . . I really appreciate the values she cherishes. She has a lot of very good values, starting from basic things like, you have to be honest in life, you have to be helpful to others. Of course, you know we are not an island. We have to be one with the community around. Both of us, of course, take so much care to help people around, you know. (Joseph, 192–93, 288–90)

Srinivas, one of the respondents, looked at certain values he and his wife hold as the main reason for the strong sense of relationship quality in their marriage. He said, "Yes, very strong support and commitment. The main supporting reason is there are values, which we are holding, and the life, which we are living. It would have been much harder, but she has adjusted very well" (Srinivas, 145–47).

Sub-theme 4: Little Instances of Love

The participants talked about how important it was to experience little instances of love from their spouses in their everyday life to make their marriage a success. Such instances often strengthened their bond and relationship. One subject, Peter, described how his wife was very concerned and caring. He said that she showed it in simple ways. "If I am away in other city, if I am gone for some other work and all, more than my parents she will call me, each and every time like, once in an hour or once in two hours or three, four times in a day, she will call. But my parents or my brothers, they will call once in a day or like once in two days like that. So, more care she is taking" (Peter, 234–38).

Another subject, Priya, referring to the love and concern she experienced from her spouse, described:

> It was my birthday last month, and I never knew but my husband had arranged for a nice greeting card, and my husband and kid, they heralded me with birthday wish which I had never anticipated, because it was the beginning of my school year for my daughter and for my college, because they were the starting days, so actually I had forgotten about my birthday, ha, ha. So that made me very happy. Yeah, a very nice card he gave me, a nice hug, he wished me my birthday, that made me very happy. And not only that, ah, he remembers even my parents' birthday, wedding anniversary and all that. And he would wish them even before I could remind him. So all those things, small things make me very happy, small gestures, which really make me happy. (Priya, 250–54)

For Aisha, one of the participants, the simple instance of travelling with her husband made her feel close to him. She said, "When I want to . . . travelling with my husband . . . I was very happy" (Aisha, 197). For Khadeejah, another participant, her husband's love was shown in the form of a little gift, and that made her very happy and close to him. She described, "In my, in our first anniversary, he bought me a gift, a glass prism. I was very happy because it is the first time that I got a gift from him" (Khadeejah, 169–70). Rose, one of the subjects, had several instances from her everyday life where she experienced the love and kindness of her husband. She said:

> Recently also I had another fall. I feel because I am hefty, I was walking to my sister-in-law's place. And by mistake I missed step, I took a step forward, and I strained my leg. Then I was again bedridden. Then he was so much caring. Then I felt that I am really gifted to have such a loving person. So what should I do for him? I didn't have words to tell. Though both my parents are no more, but I feel, really they did the, took the nice decision of getting me a good husband, who is so much caring. He is always caring. Always, though he goes a little late to the office also he sees that I have, everything is provided for me, and everything is brought to me, on to my table. And [he] tells me to take everything, and

entrusts me to somebody, and only then he goes. So I don't know. All that caring is something that I can never forget. I always pray for him, always pray to give him good health. (Rose, 219–29)

For one subject, Thomas, the kindness and understanding of his wife came in the form of some financial help when he was going through a difficult time financially. "I had some financial problems. I needed one lakh thirty thousand (one hundred and thirty thousand rupees). I did not have sufficient money. And she gave me her gold to mortgage. But that happened last week. And I was very happy and I, it is very difficult to get money from other sources. I had sources, but for them also it was difficult, my friends. And she was ready to give, mortgage her gold. I was very happy" (Thomas, 156–60).

Arpitha, another subject, had several instances where she experienced the tenderness and love of her husband in her everyday life. She described one of those instances as follows:

I think last week itself, ah, I don't know, these days, I have a lot of ah, feet pain. So I was too tired of late. My health was not that good. So I slept off. And I think in my sleep I was flattering, or what do you say, I was just feeling the pain. My husband was working there. So he came and he was literally pressing my feet to comfort myself. And then only after sometime I realized and I said, when I woke up he gave me a tablet. I took the tablet, made me wait for a few minutes. He takes care of me. Then I have some, when I was feeling bad, why these things are happening. I have prescriptions. So, he took the prescriptions and got the medicine. Yes. I got the medicines, he said. (Arpitha, 280–89)

Sub-theme 5: Religion and Spirituality

Indians, in general, are very religious, and that factor was reflected in many of the interviews. The participants indicated that their religious beliefs were an important factor in strengthening their marital bond and family life. One subject, Priya, shared about her beliefs and their role in her family life:

See, basically, religion, yeah, we have to follow certain rule, but not only my husband. Personally, I believe that; I don't believe all that elaborate puja [Hindu services] and rituals and all that, because everything is man made, some five thousand years back. But to some extent I believe that if we are good, good things will happen to us and our kids. . . . And we both are, actually we both are interested in these spiritual things, though we don't follow, we like to go to discourse together, or he reads Bhagavat Gita, he may be reciting, I may join him, so we have ah, ah, eh, interest in same things, most of the things or especially spiritual things. It is not like that we are still young we don't want to go into that and all that, we both are interested. (Priya, 287–90)

Peter, another subject, said that he and his wife were very religious, and their religious practices were helpful in building up their relationship. He reflected on this theme and said:

To be very frank, I can't attend mass every day and say the prayers every day. When I am working I don't get time for that. She [wife] says rosary every day and she says the prayers, but I attend only on the weekends. On every Saturday, we pray the rosary together. Yes, it is very important. Religion, like, it's my family background. Everyone is very religious and that is my background. I also believe in all that. But I don't show it off, like I do all these things and all that. I definitely believe, and religion is very important. (Peter, 161–66)

Rose, another participant, described how she and her family took their religious practices very seriously. She reported:

My husband is very much particular about the religion. He is very, he says, whatever it is, without religion we don't have anything. He is very particular that every Sunday we go to church, very particular that we go on time. And he is very particular that we also go to church . . . go on time. Our parish, to go to our parish, we have to take two buses. But he says, whatever it is, the only way is to spend with the Lord. We should thank the Lord for what he has given us. If it was not his blessings, we cannot live this day. (Rose, 303–17)

Thomas, one of the participants, likewise had something similar to say about the importance of religion and religious practices in his family life. "Religion is very important, not only for a Christian. I give more importance to values. Values are very important, for the growth in our childhood. We study these values from our church. I give more importance to that. And in the family also, I teach them values. We have our prayer, prayer session, daily evening prayer, daily we spend some time, evening, we [have] prayer session" (Thomas, 242–46).

The responses and comments of the subjects thus show that there were many things that they considered as the most important elements in making their marital relationships healthy and happy.

THEME 4: ASSESSMENT OF MARITAL RELATIONSHIP

The different dimensions of marital relationship, which were also the focus of this study, were discussed and assessed specifically in all the interviews. The participants shared their experiences about each of these dimensions. Overall, they described their relationship as happy and positive. One participant had a very negative experience with regard to her marriage and relationship with her spouse. However, she reported that she would put her husband first when it came to ranking the significant people in her life. A description of the various aspects of the participants' marital relationship is given in the following sections.

Sub-theme 1: Satisfaction

All the participants, except one, said that they were very satisfied in their marital relationship. There were a couple of them who said that they were satisfied, but they hoped that their partners would give them a little more attention. One subject, Joseph, had only positive things to say about his marriage and relationship with his wife. He stated:

> I am really happy. It is a very happy and successful marriage. . . .
> When I look back, I had a very wonderful married life, you see.
> During the wedding, after marriage, after children were born, after
> the children are gone from home, all the time, I had a wonder-
> ful marriage. Even when we go to visit them [children], they see
> that. We stay with them and help them with their needs. We have
> enjoyed that kind of family life, and our children learn from that.
> That has really helped us. . . . I am really happy. It is a very happy
> and successful marriage. . . . Imagine of course, it is almost forty
> or thirty-nine years of married life. After all, our fist son, you see,
> is thirty-eight. And you know what he told my second son at the
> time of his marriage? He said, "I don't want to give you any piece of
> advice, but you just follow what your parents did." I was so happy
> to hear that. He openly said that. (Joseph, 152–59, 437–42)

Jaya, another subject, described her marriage as generally happy and that she was satisfied. However, she said that they were not free from problems. She said, "We are happy. Some problems, misunderstanding, problems, individual problems are there. But we have a strong marriage" (Jaya, 98–99). Rose, one of the participants, described her marriage as very happy and satisfying. She reported, "We have very happy and nice married life.

My husband is a very nice, understanding person. That's what I told you. The only thing we lack is money. But other than that, we are happy. He takes good care of me. Though he doesn't clothe himself, he sees that I clothe well, fed well, feed my children" (Rose, 100–103).

Renuka, one of the subjects, rated her marriage as happy and successful saying, "Happy, happy married life" (Renuka, 34). Priya, another subject, described her marriage as very satisfying. "We are almost like friends, more than husband and wife. Very happy with my relationship" (Priya, 57–58). Another participant, Kavya, had similar sentiments about her marriage. "If I analyze my family life, I would say, I was satisfied, I am satisfied, I would say" (Kavya, 146–47). Arpitha, another participant, was all positive and excited about her marriage. "Pretty happy, on top of the world. And completely satisfied" (Arpitha, 61).

One subject, Aisha, reported that she was satisfied in her marriage but she would love a little more freedom. Her in-laws have a lot of influence on their day-to-day affairs, and that appeared to be a constant irritant for her. She stated, "I enjoy in this marriage life because I get help from my husband, I get love from my husband. I get everything from him. But I don't get much freedom, because, if I want to go somewhere, if I want to do something, I should ask them, his parents. Please give . . . I have to ask everybody in the family. So, I don't get much freedom" (Aisha, 86–90).

Khadeejah, another respondent, considered her marriage as happy and satisfying. However, she reported that her husband was very busy with his work, taking care of his parents, and engaging in social and charitable activities. She said that he would make a lot of sacrifices and spend a lot of time to help others, but that had some negative impact on their marital life as he could not be available to her as and when she needed. She said, "He considers others more . . . about his family, more than his family, he [is] concerned [about] others, about the poor, poor persons, poor people in the society. He likes social service very much" (Khadeejah, 39–41).

Overall, the results from the qualitative interviews suggest that the subjects have a very strong sense of satisfaction, which, in turn, contributes significantly to their relationship quality.

Sub-theme 2: Quality of Alternatives

The majority of the participants in the phenomenological interviews indicated that they viewed their current relationship as the best in reference to other alternatives (another partner, friends, family). To state it differently, their current marital relationships fulfilled their most important needs, and they could not think of anyone else that would fulfill those needs as best as they have it now. The responses of many of the participants confirmed this theme. One of the subjects, Joseph, said, "If I were to marry again, you know I will marry the same person. I will marry because, I don't think there is anybody else in this world as good as her" (Joseph, 483–86). At several stages during the interview, Joseph explained why his wife was the best who could fulfill his most important needs. He said, "I am so lucky. She is very intelligent . . . she is really beautiful . . . she is hard working . . . she is very faithful to me" (Joseph, 196, 268, 350, 360). Kavya, another participant, had similar feelings about her marriage and husband. She stated:

> We can't simply think about it as romantic. I won't consider that my life is so romantic, but I feel that I am satisfied with my life. I feel and I cannot imagine someone else marrying me. Maybe I may find somebody who has got slight similarities, but I don't think, I can't expect someone else would come and marry me and I will lead such a kind of life and all, I can't . . . Because he never, you know, gives me pressure. He has not asked me to go for a job. He says, if you want to go, you go, that is your interest. And he has never forced me to take up the job here, like he wants me to be with him. But he says, if you want to go for a job in Kerala, you go there, but I will miss you a lot. He would say that. So, I know what he wants and he knows what I want. (Kavya, 179–83, 200–204)

Srinivas, one of the subjects, said that he was very satisfied in his relationship with his wife, and he considered her as the best person in his life who could fulfill his most important needs. He said, "I think, at present, yes, I put her first. . . . I am not saying that I had the highest moral or anything like that. The thing is, my wife was there and that was sufficient for me. I love her" (Srinivas, 288–89). Another participant, Priya, expressed similar feelings. "I am ready to sacrifice anything for this relationship" (Priya, 217–18). Rose, one of the subjects, sounded very attached to her husband, and could not imagine another person coming in his place. She stated, "Yes, my husband is the most important. Even though all these things have to go away, I am ready, but I will not let go my husband" (Rose, 275–76).

Venkatesh, one of the subjects, saw his marriage as the best that he could have had because it helped him to become disciplined and committed. He said, "Marriage brings a disciplined life. . . . After my marriage, I became a little more disciplined. Before marriage, there was no responsibility or discipline" (Venkatesh, 148–50).

The theme of shared values and responsibilities also was related to this theme of the quality of alternatives. The majority of the participants felt that their current marital relationship was the best because of the shared values and responsibilities as well. Renuka, one of the subjects, shared that her husband consulted her before making any decision, and he helped her with household chores. She said, "Yeah, he consults. For each and everything he consults. . . . Yeah, everything, household work, cleaning, and everything . . . daily he will help me" (Renuka, 138). Joseph, one of the subjects, said that in addition to sharing the household chores and child care, he and his wife shared many values and principles in common, and that contributed to their relationship quality. He stated:

> We always believe in sharing, sharing in the sense, you know, at home we share, the household chores we share, about taking care of children, we shared. There was no complaint. . . . I really appreciate the values she cherishes. She has a lot of very good values, starting from basic things like, you have to be honest in life, you have to be helpful to others. Of course, you know we are not an island, we have to be one with the community around. Both of us, of course, take so much care to help people around, you know. When guests come, people, relatives come, we go an extra mile, to make sure that they are comfortable and, of course, they stay. That is the case with both of us. That is why in the beginning I said, our values, you know, they are, they are, same, more or less. (Joseph, 192–93, 288–90)

The results from the qualitative interviews thus indicate that for the majority of the subjects, their present marital relationship is the best that they could have had in meeting the most important needs of their life, and that feeling helps the development of their relationship quality. Other alternatives that would offer better possibilities to meet those needs are either nil or weaker in comparison with what they have now.

Sub-theme 3: Investment of Resources

All the participants said that their marriages were marked by high level of investments. Their investments included money and materials, time and talents, decision to have children together, and emotional support and relationships. One subject, Priya, reported that her contributions were more in terms of time, talents, and emotional support. She stated, "Money-wise, my investment is zero. He [husband] was invested [financially], but all other things, emotions, love, everything, time, both of us have done it" (Priya, 202–3). Venkatesh, another participant, said that his contribution to the marriage in the beginning stage of their marital relationship was in terms of allowing his wife to get educated and get a job. He reported:

> And I make my wife to study further and she got, when I got marriage [married], she passed only pre-university degree. Then she got graduation. And post graduation, and B Ed also. So after-wards, we got a job, and in that way, economically I helped like that. Yes. Financially we both are helpful. I always encouraged. And ah, because my side [family] was a little bit weaker in eco-nomical situation, sometimes I used to help my brother, and there was no second thought from her side. She is supportive. To live a peaceful life up to the grave, and other things are as usual, day-to-day spending time, everything, living in house. Yeah, we have a satisfactory job, not a very high job, but satisfied in my job, and she is also very satisfied in her job. More than that, she is more a hard worker than me. (Venkatesh, 64–84)

Thomas, one of the subjects, shared that like him his wife also had in-vested much into their relationship. He cited one example to show how much his wife was investing into the relationship. She willingly gave him her gold and ornaments when he needed some money. He reported, "I had some fi-nancial problems. I needed one lakh thirty thousand (one hundred and thirty thousand rupees). I did not have sufficient money. And she gave me her gold to mortgage" (Thomas, 156–58). For Jaya and Joseph, two of the subjects, investments also meant spouses allowing each other to become friends with their friends. Jaya said, "Almost all his friends are my friends" (Jaya, 464). Joseph said something similar, "My colleagues and friends are, of course, her colleagues and friends. . . . Good profession, money of course, security, and then children, all those things do help" (Joseph, 377, 433–34).

Mary, one of the participants, who has an alcoholic husband, said that in spite of her husband's wastefulness, she had invested much into the rela-tionship, taking care of him and taking care of the needs of her family. She described it as follows:

> Whatever we need, I have to buy. For him also, I have to buy. For my child also I have to buy. Whatever he is spending, he is spend-ing for his friends. And he has got hundred rupees and if someone

asks him two hundred rupees, he will go and get from some other person and give that two hundred rupees for this friend. And the friends, they won't give back. If I ask, he will say, "no need to ask, this is my money." . . . When he drinks he gets migraine. Then he started to vomit. That's why he stopped. His liver, one side is already gone (damaged), doctor said. When I took him to the neurologist, he took x-ray, scanning, and all that. (Mary, 152–56)

The overall results from the phenomenological interviews show that all the subjects had invested much into their relationships in terms of money, materials, time, and emotional support, and that helped them to strengthen their marital relationship.

Sub-theme 4: Intimacy

The majority of the participants expressed the view that intimacy was a very important contributor to the quality of their marital relationship. They reported that they were very close to their spouses and longed to spend more time with them. Joseph, one of the participants, shared that he and his wife very rarely stayed away from each other. When they had to do it for some reason, they missed each other a great deal. He stated, "We always, even if we have to go away, you know, the other day, my wife had to go to my first son's place, to take care of their son. But every time she goes, I will be waiting for her to come back. We miss each other; yes, we miss each other. And, of course, we crave for, you know, for that moment when we come back" (Joseph, 282–87).

Priya, another respondent, reflected back on some of her early experiences and found instances where her husband did little things that made her feel very close to him. She said:

I think he loves me a lot because, ah, first time when we have been to an outing before our marriage, we had been to a movie and all that, he had taken me for dinner and all that, that day, the tissue paper I had used, he had kept it with him, he had written the date, this is the first time I had been with my wife, and also until date he preserves the rose which he was wearing on his reception coat, and not only that, the ticket with which he travelled from Mysore to Hassan when my daughter was born, that first day ticket, he still preserves it. (Priya, 74–80)

Kavya, one of the participants, shared that there was a lot of trust between her and her husband, and that strengthened their bond and intimacy. She reported:

> For me, intimacy is openness. We may fight, but we speak openly when I feel angry or when I feel sad, or when I feel happiness, I have to express it out to somebody, and my husband is there at home. He will be the first one to receive it. But there are a few things which I would like to share with my friends first and then with him. There are a few things, which I would like to share with my parent or my sister, or even my sister-in-law, and later I will transfer it to him. But, you know, I am so close to him in the sense, I have the openness, or I can talk to him anything in this world, even if I tell him that I want to have an extra-marital relationship with someone else, or I have seen the person and love him, he will not prevent me. That's what he [is], that's what I feel. So, if I have got that openness with him, because he won't take it in any other sense. (Kavya, 300–310)

Arpitha, another subject, described her relationship with her husband as very personal and private and it was not something to show to others. She said that she had the freedom to talk to him about anything that she had on her mind. She also said that their intimacy was felt even in simple gestures such as looking at each other. She described it in the following words:

> Spending some personal time with each other . . . it doesn't mean, intimacy means sitting together always or anything. So, whenever we get time, ah, we take a day off or when we get a day off, both of us go out to have lunch or dinner, sit alone. . . . So, intimacy means to me, it is not a show to the outer world, that we are close and all that. Understanding internally, even the looks what we give to each other, we know that we are intimate. . . . Initially at the time of my marriage, I am very soft going person. So, if I have to convey something, which is harsh or something, I used to shiver, and immediately get tears and all that. And it was completely the other way with my husband. He cannot bear someone crying for something, simple things. It is something, which he could not accept. So, I was not in a position to communicate with him. So, there were times during those days I used to like, remain, putting walls. Because once it starts I end up crying, not actually communicating what has to be communicated. And I used to get scared maybe in that emotion, I may speak something wrong, which will,

> ah, start some problem in our relationship. So, for one thing, ten
> times, I will write up and read, and rethink about what I have writ-
> ten whether it is correct or how the message can be passed to him.
> And then send him the message. That was the five years, six years
> back, the last mail I wrote to him. Now I don't have such problems.
> Anything I can talk to him personally, and it will end, he takes it in
> a positive way. (Arpitha, 195–219)

Peter, another subject, reported that his relationship with his wife had
grown to a higher level of friendship. He described it as, "Still we are like
friends. Her mom and all will tell, give him respect, and all that, not calling
with name and all that (in some communities in India, addressing one's
husband by name is considered disrespectful). She sometimes calls me as
if my friend is calling, by name, like friends call, with friends' initials and
all that" (Peter, 186–89). For one participant, Mary, growing in intimacy,
however, was not an easy task. She reported, "If he is not drinking I am very
happy. No need [of] house, no need of finance or wealth. Only one thing I
want is, he should stop drinking" (Mary, 304–5).

The comments and observations of the majority of the subjects demonstrate that intimacy is a deeply felt variable in their marital relationships,
and it helps to improve the quality of their relationship.

Sub-theme 5: Passion

Reflecting on the theme of passion, most of the subjects expressed that they
were very passionate about their partners and relationships. In reference to
this dimension of marriage, some participants talked about the importance
of sex and other expressions of love, while others talked of going beyond
sex and sexual expressions. One subject, Joseph, stated that he was very
passionate about his wife and could not imagine a life without her. He
reported that he and his wife expressed their passionate feelings for each
other in various ways. He described it as follows:

> Sexual attraction for each other has also played a major role in our
> relationship. Both of us are healthy and our health has never come
> in the way. Sometimes, you know, when my friends say that this is
> coming in the way because of this or that, I feel that this has never
> come in our way. . . . Certainly, kissing, yes, even the look, you
> know. That's right. God has, of course, given us wonderful organs
> like eyes, you know. They are very powerful, and of course, other
> things automatically follow. If I were to marry again, I will marry

the same person. I will marry because I don't think there is any-body else in this world as good as her. (Joseph, 145–46, 322–24, 485–86)

Priya, another subject, shared her thoughts and experiences regarding the theme of passion in similar lines. She reported that she and her husband have bonded so well that she would choose him as her husband if they were reborn. She said, "We find our sexual relationship satisfactory. But compared to the beginning years of our marriage, maybe the frequency has come down, but still whenever we have, we are happy with it. Basically, I don't believe in punarjanma [rebirth] and all that, and if I am given a chance, yes, I will marry him again" (Priya, 179–80).

Srinivas, one of the respondents, described his sense of passion in his marital relationship in the following words: "That [sex] is one of the best things we have" (Srinivas, 202). Similarly, Peter, another subject, shared that sex was very important in their life. He said, "We gave importance to sexual life, so we got a kid within one year after marriage, giving importance to sexual life" (Peter, 260–61). Arpitha, another participant, said that she and her husband had a very satisfying sexual relationship:

> Actually to have such good marital life, I strongly think that both of us are interested in sex. And mostly, ah, he is into more, ah, like to initiate, rather than, I am also, whether interested or not, we get along very well. So, it is in a very good ways for both of us. So absolutely, he initiates it and that's fine. Even though having kids and other things, we try to have our own space. He understands me completely. If I am not keeping well or anything, he just understands. And even other ways, if I see that he really wants it, I compromise and we have sex. So it is mutual. There is absolutely no force or anything like that. . . . Actually, in this sense I should say that initially, for the first one year, we had a problem in our sexual relationship. Because I was not aware of many things, I was not educated in those ways. . . . And in our culture, they don't even educate you. So, similar background he had come from. So, then I got pregnant immediately which I didn't expect. Unfortunately got aborted. Then for one year I had many issues, like I used to always cry and I struggled for one year. After my son was born, and after that it was fine. (Arpitha, 166–87)

One participant, Khadeejah, reported that for her, although sex was important, it was not the most important thing in her marriage. She stated, "Our married life is not mainly meant for that. But it also makes us happy"

(Khadeejah, 187–88). There were a couple of participants who did not feel very excited or passionate about their partners. Jaya, one of the subjects, sounded somewhat dissatisfied that her husband was not interested in having sex. But she appeared to be rationalizing it by considering sex as not the most important thing. She described it as follows:

> Actually, I want to tell you one thing. We have not had sex for almost fifteen years, maybe in 1996 or 1998. . . . He could not have that physical relationship. At that time, he wrote a letter and I read. And then I said, this is not the permanent thing, eh, so don't worry about that. . . . He has diabetes. I think it is because of that. Maybe he saw the doctors also. I don't know about that. No, he tried, but it was not successful, it was not successful. That is the thing. He is seventy, I am sixty-six. I already said that it is important, part and parcel of a good marriage. I agree. But it is not the most important thing. . . . He is very supportive, but again, his nature is that he does not show affection outside. You asked that question about touching or kissing or things like that in your questionnaire. There is nothing like that. He doesn't do all that. . . . One more thing I will tell you. So, maybe recently, maybe three or four years like that, both of us are not sleeping together. Once I said, "Why are you doing like that? Why don't we sleep together?" But I don't know, he sleeps separately, I don't know. (Jaya, 272–325)

Mary, one of the participants, shared that she was not interested in having sex with her husband as he often came home inebriated and violent. She reported it as follows:

> If he wants to sleep with me, he has to come without drinking. Otherwise, I won't allow. I don't like the smell. In that case, I am very strict. Because of that only, he is getting more angry, I think. I told him in the morning, if you want to sleep with me, you come without drinking. Otherwise I won't allow. The smell, I don't like. . . . We have no sex at all. . . . Even on the first day, that day itself he was fully drunk. Actually, if I was in my house, I would have run away from there. . . . We are not sleeping together. And I don't want to sleep with him also now. I am not interested also. Truly I can say I don't want it. Even in the first night also he is not enjoying with me all that. I am not interested. We are not feeling like kissing or hugging and all that. If he is behaving in the proper way, we feel something. We don't feel all that. (Mary, 250–86)

The majority of the subjects in the study reported that passion was a strongly felt variable in their marriages, and that, in turn, helped to improve the quality of their relationships. However, it appeared that a few of the subjects (e.g., Khadeejah) did not want to give too much importance to this variable in marriage.

Sub-theme 6: Commitment

Given the fact that Indians, in general, consider faithfulness to one's marital partner as a sacred duty, it was not surprising to hear all the participants saying that they were very committed in their marriages and would do their best to keep the relationships going. Not all the participants were happy with their marriages (e.g., Mary), but none of them indicated that they would do anything that would weaken their commitment to their partners. One of the respondents, Joseph, was very strong and specific about his marital commitment and faithfulness to his wife. He stated:

> Thirty-nine or almost forty years of marriage, it continues to be there. It is very important. That's why, I can tell you, never, never we have deviated from that oath, that oath that have taken at the time of our marriage. That has never, never, by any chance, it has not come. So there was no, no, I should not say, even that word, or what you call, extra-marital relationship, never it has happened. Of course, we are faithful to each other. Of course, we have lived away from each other, only for ten or fifteen days all of our married life. Isn't that great? We always, even if we have to go away, you know, the other day, my wife had to go to my first son's place, to take care of their son. But every time she goes, I will be waiting for her to come back. (Joseph, 273–79)

Another respondent, Jaya, stated that she did not even like to entertain any thought about being unfaithful to her husband. She said, "No I don't like. Someone asked me why don't you have anything like that. But I don't like that. That is not permanent. I don't like. So I don't like all those things" (Jaya, 448–51). Talking about her commitment to her husband, another participant, Priya, said, "I am ready to sacrifice anything for this relationship" (Priya, 217–18). According to Srinivas, another subject, the main reason for the strong sense of commitment in his marriage is the values that he and his wife hold. He said, "Yes, very strong support and commitment. The main supporting reason is, there are values, which we are holding, and the life, which we are living. It would have been much harder, but she has adjusted very well" (Srinivas, 145–47).

One of the subjects, Mary, reported that her marriage was unhappy and unsatisfying. She reported that her alcoholic husband used to engage in violence and beat her. However, she did not think of leaving him or replacing him with anybody else. She said, "No, whatever he may be, he is still my husband. He will be the first" (Mary, 332).

The overall results thus show that the subjects in the present study have a strong feeling of commitment. They view commitment as a sacred duty and remain faithful to their spouses. The majority of the subjects appeared to suggest that their strong sense of commitment contributed to strengthening their marriages and improving the quality of their relationships.

THEME 5: PERSISTENCE IN MARRIAGE AS A PRIORITY

Persistence was found to be a highly valued component of the subjects' marital relationships. All the participants indicated that they would do everything possible to persist in their marriage. Even those who said that it was tough or hard to adjust with their partners indicated that they would continue their marriages at all costs. One of the subjects, Mary, whose husband is an alcoholic and abusive, said:

> I used to tell him always, "whatever you do to me in all way, but I still love you very much, because you are the one person who chose me." So, whatever it is, it is okay. No problem, if he beats me also, no problem, I am happy. One week, there was mark here (scar on face), they [her brothers] asked me whether. . . . they will think so much of stories. But I didn't say anything. But still I like him very much. I don't want to leave him. If something happens to him, my life is gone. Whatever it is, I love him. I remember my mummy. She was always very loving and forgiving. I don't want anything that is different. It is because of the marriage vows. I have given myself to him, and I have promised to love him no matter what. (Mary, 338–61)

Another subject, Jaya, said that she had difficulties in adjusting with some of the behaviors of her husband. Sometimes she felt excluded from his company. But she persevered and continued to remain faithful. She described her experience in the following words: "He wants to travel more with his friends. When I was working, at that time, I gave preference to work. Work is worship, that is the way. I worked very sincerely. So, he used to travel, maybe fifteen days, or a month, just like that. Yeah, away from home. Even though I never complained. So that is his nature. Sometimes, I felt it tough" (Jaya, 245–49).

Arpitha, another participant, said that it was very difficult for her in the beginning of her marriage. But she persisted. She described her experience as follows:

> And my mother-in-law is very aggressive and short tempered, which had created a lot of issues in our marriage. She was having very high expectations, few things, communication gap, and it was really bad. I was really scared the time when they sent off, like, in our thing [community/culture], we have a formal send off, where father will hand over the girl to the in-laws, and say, that's it, our obligations are over. So, from there I was really tensed. But the minute I came to my husband, he was the person who was comforting me, and he has taken care. So I didn't have any issues, only slight disturbances, I think, with any family this might be there, with respect to my mother-in-law. But I never spoke back to her. So even though he was a little bit towards his parents he slowly started. I think it took three to four years by the time he started understanding me, with respect to in-laws also. (Arpitha, 47–58)

The responses from the subjects thus demonstrate a strong sense of sacredness of their marriages and a felt need to persist in their marital relationships. Although some of them were not very happy with their relationships (e.g., Mary), they felt that they had a duty to persevere in their commitments and remain faithful to their spouses.

All the themes that were generated from the phenomenological interviews and discussed here revealed rich facts about this sample's assessment of their marital relationships. Overall, the majority of the subjects felt that they had very healthy and strong marital relationships. A detailed discussion of both the quantitative and qualitative results is done in Part V.

PART V

Discussion and Interpretation

13

Summary and Discussion of the Findings

THIS CHAPTER PRESENTS WHAT LeCompte and Schensul (2013) called "the process of putting together all the pieces" of the study and transforming them "into a full story" (p. 265). First, the chapter presents a summary of the findings of this study. Then the findings of the study are discussed in detail, specifically, looking into the results obtained from the analysis of both the quantitative and qualitative data.

The discussion primarily focuses on the main topic of the study, relationship quality, and its six associated variables: satisfaction, quality of alternatives, investments, intimacy, passion, and commitment. For each of these variables, the findings from the quantitative data are summarized and discussed first, and then the researcher supplements those findings with themes generated from the qualitative data. Quotes and comments from the subjects are cited to show how the qualitative findings support and supplement the quantitative results. The chapter also discusses findings regarding gender and additional themes that emerged from the qualitative interviews that were related to the topic of the study but not covered under the quantitative measures.

SUMMARY OF THE STUDY

The purpose of this study was to explore the relationship quality in arranged marriages in India. The overall results from both the quantitative and qualitative data revealed that in this sample of the arranged marriages in India, the relationship quality was positive and high. For the question on the overall relationship quality of their marriages, 282 (98.3 percent) out of the 287 subjects rated their relationship as positive.

The research questions that directed this study also explored whether the relationship quality in arranged marriages in India was associated with marital satisfaction, quality of alternatives, investment of resources, intimacy, passion, and commitment. As hypothesized, the study results indicated a statistically significant positive correlation between relationship quality and satisfaction, investments, intimacy, passion, and commitment, and a negative correlation between relationship quality and quality of alternatives. The subjects confirmed that these variables were significant factors in their marital relationships.

The multiple linear regression results showed that the added factors of marital satisfaction, quality of alternatives, investment of resources, intimacy, passion, and commitment could account for 59.9 percent of the variance of factors that contribute to the relationship quality in this sample. Consistent with the existing literature and studies done with other populations, the current study established that the more satisfaction, investments, intimacy, passion, and commitment, and less alternatives the subjects have in their marriages, the higher will be their relationship quality.

The sense of high relationship quality and its associated factors were also reflected in the results obtained from the phenomenological interviews. The five major themes that were generated from the qualitative data—family involvement, limited premarital contact, essential elements for success, assessment of marital relationship, and persistence in marriage as a priority—were consistent with the quantitative findings.

DISCUSSION OF THE FINDINGS

One of the drawbacks of most of the studies done on arranged marriages in India in the past was that they had used a quantitative-only method, which failed to fully capture the lived experience of the participants. This might have been one of the reasons for the conflicting reports in the literature about marital relationship in such marriages. In that regard, the current study was much more in-depth, capturing more fully the lived experience of the participants. The following section discusses in detail the findings of both the quantitative and qualitative data in this study, and shows where and how the convergence or differences of the two data sets occurred.

Relationship Quality

Both the quantitative and qualitative results showed that the respondents of this study had healthy and happy marital relationships. For a general question on the quality of their marital relationship, 98 percent of the respondents rated the overall quality of their marital relationship as positive. This is a much higher percentage of relationship quality than the results found in some of the studies done on marriages of choice and romantic relationships. For example, Katz and Lavee (2005) cited a study done by Shaked who found that among Jewish men and women in Israel, 74 percent of men and 61 percent of women were very satisfied with their marital relationship. The percentage of marital happiness or relationship quality found in the current study is also higher than those found in some of the previous studies done on arranged marriages in India. For example, Sandhya (2009) assessed marital happiness, intimacy, good times, and conflict among couples in arranged marriages in India. Overall, 94 percent of the couples in that study reported being happy in their marriages.

Replicating the findings of Rusbult et al. (1998) and Sternberg (1986), the current study indicated that there was a significant association between relationship quality and satisfaction, quality of alternatives, investments, intimacy, passion, and commitment in this sample. The multiple linear regression analysis, in fact, showed that about 60 percent of the variance in this sample's relationship quality could be explained by the combined influence of satisfaction, quality of alternatives, investments, intimacy, passion, and commitment. Such significant associations between these variables, according to Rusbult et al. (1998) and Sternberg (1986), indicated higher functioning in relationships. The themes generated from the responses of the participants in the qualitative interviews were consistent with the quantitative findings regarding the different study variables and their associations. The themes captured the subjects' experience and assessment of their marital relationships. The following sections will discuss each of the six independent variables and demonstrate how they were associated with the subjects' relationship quality.

Satisfaction

Specifically looking into the level of satisfaction in this sample, the mean scores and the correlation results indicated that the subjects in this sample had a strong sense of satisfaction, and this variable was significantly associated with their relationship quality. These quantitative findings were supported and supplemented by the results obtained from the qualitative interviews. Several themes that were generated from the qualitative data were related to the variable of satisfaction. Themes such as family involvement, shared values and responsibilities, beliefs and practices with regard to religion and spirituality, little instances of love in everyday life, acceptance and understanding, adjustments and compromises, quality of alternatives, investments, intimacy, passion, commitment, and persistence in marriage as a priority were all tied into the subjects' marital satisfaction. Specifically, the theme of satisfaction itself captured the subjects' thoughts and feelings about the level of satisfaction in their marriages. Indicating this high sense of satisfaction in this sample, one of the subjects, Joseph, for example, said, "I am really happy . . . during the wedding, after marriage, after children were born, after the children are gone from home, all the time, I had a wonderful marriage" (Joseph, 152–54, 437–48).

Bradbury et al. (2000), in their review of a decade's research on marital satisfaction, stated that marital satisfaction was probably the single most important factor in understanding the quality of marriage. In the current study, looking at both the quantitative and qualitative responses from the subjects, it can be stated that the satisfaction variable indeed was an important factor that positively influenced their relationship quality. Etcheverry et al. (2012) opined that the overall sense of satisfaction in a relationship (positive or negative) depends on the rewards and costs associated with the relationship. In relationships that have high satisfaction, rewards are high and costs are few. Looking at the quantitative and qualitative responses from the subjects in this sample, specifically, high mean scores on the satisfaction scale of the IMS and the theme of satisfaction, it can be noticed that these relationships were high in rewards and low in costs.

These results of the current study concerning marital satisfaction that contributed to the subject's relationship quality were consistent with the findings of some of the past studies done on arranged marriages in India. Several studies had reported a high level of marital satisfaction in arranged marriages in India (Chawla, 2007; Madathil and Benshoff, 2008; Sandhya, 2009; Yelsma and Athappilly, 1988).

Quality of Alternatives

Referring to the role of the quality of alternatives in the overall functioning in relationship settings, Rusbult et al. (1998) and others (e.g., Etcheverry et al., 2013; Macher, 2013; Rodrigues and Lopes, 2013) suggested that when the quality of alternatives is high, the relationship quality tends to be low. These authors refer to this variable in terms of a person choosing to stay with a relationship because it fulfills his or her most important needs. In other words, if a person has better alternatives outside the current relationship, his or her dependence on the partner will be less, and consequently the relationship quality will be weaker. If alternatives are readily available, the person will not feel the need to depend on the partner, and consequently the relationship quality will decline (Panayiotou, 2005). On the other hand, if the alternatives outside the current relationship are fewer, he or she will feel the need to depend on the partner more, and that will strengthen the relationship quality. In other words, if the desired outcomes are not available in other relationships, it means that there are fewer alternatives to the current relationship (Etcheverry et al., 2012).

Although several studies have been done on arranged marriages in India, the variable of quality of alternatives was still a largely unexplored area. The current study, in both the quantitative and qualitative formats, revealed that for the majority of the subjects in this sample, their present marital relationship was the best that they could have had in meeting the most important needs of their life. The mean scores obtained for the quality of alternatives in the current study indicated low quality of alternatives, which meant that for the majority of the subjects, their current marital relationship was the best in reference to other alternatives (another partner, friends, family). To state it differently, their current marital relationships fulfilled their most important needs and no one else could have fulfilled those needs as well as they have it now. This sense of their current relationship as the best choice they could have had in fulfilling their most important needs was positively correlated with their relationship quality.

The quantitative findings were also reflected in the findings from the qualitative data. The theme, assessment of marital relationship, and its subtheme on the quality of alternatives captured the feelings and thoughts of the subjects regarding the quality of alternatives in their marital life. The responses of the majority of the participants in the phenomenological interviews indicated that they viewed their current relationship as the best in reference to other alternatives (another partner, friends, family). In other words, their current marital relationships fulfilled their most important needs, and they could not think of another relationship or setting that would have fulfilled those needs as well as their marriage. For example, one of the participants, Kavya, expressed her feelings about this theme of alternatives and described how she thought of her husband as the best person to fulfill her most important needs. She stated, "I cannot imagine someone else marrying me. Maybe I may find somebody who has got slight similarities, but I don't think I will lead such a kind of life and all" (Kavya, 179–83).

The literature has shown that most of the marital alliances in India were finalized only after ensuring that most of the demands and expectations of both parties were met. These expectations could include things such as similarity of both families in their socioeconomic status, caste, religion, and family traditions, the physical complexion and attractiveness of the bride and groom, geographical distance between families, dowry, match of horoscopes, and education. Attending to these details and ensuring that most of them are satisfactorily met before marriage could be a reason why the subjects felt that their current relationship was the best they could have had in fulfilling their most important needs.

Thus, consistent with the basic assumptions of the investment model, the current study, both in the quantitative and qualitative formats, found that the subjects perceived the quality of alternatives to be low or weak because they found their current relationships as the best to fulfill their most important needs. The low quality of alternatives, in turn, is shown in this study to be positively correlated with their relationship quality, as the theory suggested.

Investments

The investment model suggested that because people invest a great deal into their relationships, in terms of time, money, energy, emotional support, and other resources, it would be too costly and damaging if people were to end their relationships (Etcheverry et al., 2012; Panayiotou, 2005; Rusbult et al., 1998). The authors suggested that when partners invest so much into their relationship, their investment automatically works as a "psychological inducement" (Rusbult et al., 1998, p. 3) to depend on each other and strengthen their marital bond and relationship. In the current study, both the quantitative and qualitative findings showed that all the subjects had invested a great deal into their relationships in terms of money, materials, time, and emotional support.

The results showed a high mean score for investments, and the correlation results indicated a significant correlation between their investments and relationship quality. The investments the subjects made appeared to help their interdependence, and that, in turn, helped to strengthen their marital relationships as the investment model suggested. Authors who have studied Indian society and arranged marriages in India (e.g., Chacko, 2003; Jacobson, 1996; Singh, 2005) have found that interdependence is a basic feature of the collectivistic Indian society. Interdependence solidifies family and community relationships in India. It is assumed that the subjects in the current study already had a sense of interdependence when they came into their marriages, and their investments helped to strengthen that bond and solidify their marital relationship.

The quantitative results were again consistent with the results obtained from the qualitative interviews. The theme of investments itself captured the subjects' thoughts and feelings about how much they had invested into their relationships. For example, one subject, Priya, said that she and her husband found a good balance in their investments. She reported: "Money-wise, my investment is zero. He [husband] was invested [financially], but all other things, emotions, love, everything, time, both of us have done it" (Priya, 202–3). The theme of shared values and responsibilities also pointed to the theme of investments in the subjects' relationships. Whether doing household chores, taking care of their children, or spending time with their spouses, the subjects reported that they and their spouses had invested much into their relationships in terms of time, effort, and energy, and that, in turn, led to the strengthening of their relationships.

Rusbult et al. (1998) found that in comparison to men, women had greater investments in relationships. The quantitative results in the current study showed no significant gender difference concerning this variable. Looking into the qualitative responses of the subjects, it was difficult to discern if a difference between men or women regarding their perceptions of investment in their marital relationship existed. There were no specific themes that indicated it in either direction. The data simply confirmed that both men and women in this sample had invested a great deal in their relationship.

Intimacy

Intimacy is a feeling of closeness, bondedness, and connectedness that people experience in loving relationships (Heller and Wood, 2000; Sternberg, 1986). Both the quantitative and qualitative results in this study indicated that this sample had a strong sense of intimacy, and that, in turn, was positively related to their relationship quality. The mean scores and the correlation results indicated that the subjects in this sample had a strong sense of intimacy, and this variable was significantly associated with their relationship quality.

The quantitative findings were supported and supplemented by the themes revealed from the phenomenological interviews. The theme of intimacy captured the subjects' thoughts and feelings about their sense of intimacy in their relationships. All the participants expressed a general sense of intimacy as an emotional closeness to their spouses. However, for each of them, intimacy meant something very specific when it came to their day-to-day life. For example, for Joseph, intimacy inevitably interacted with the component of passion. He said, "We miss each other; yes, we miss each other. And of course, we crave for, you know, for, for that moment when we come back" (Joseph, 282–87).

Sternberg (1986) suggested that one of the ways to assess whether intimacy is a significant variable in relationships is to take into account how partners express their love in this area. "Without expression," Sternberg opined, "even the greatest of loves can die" (p. 132). The expression of intimacy will consist of couples or lovers communicating their inner feelings with each other, promoting each other's well-being, sharing each other's possessions, time, and self, expressing empathy for each other, and offering emotional and material support to each other (Sternberg, 1986).

In the current study, specifically in the qualitative interviews, the subjects described how intimacy was a strongly felt variable in their marital relationships and how they expressed it in their daily lives. The theme generated from descriptions of little instances of love expressed in everyday life captured this experience of the subjects. They described how the little instances of love they experienced from their spouses helped them feel close, and how the feeling of closeness, in turn, promoted their relationship quality. The majority of the subjects shared that their intimacy developed as they developed understanding and acceptance. Several of the participants identified that sharing of responsibilities and possessing common values with their spouses had helped them to grow in intimacy.

Overall, the subjects in this study reported that although they entered their marriages as virtual strangers, they had gradually become intimate partners in solid and healthy relationships. The different ways in which the participants perceived and experienced intimacy, as expressed in the qualitative interviews, were consistent with Sternberg's suggestion that intimacy could mean different things to different people. Some of these different experiences could include promotion of the welfare of the loved one, high regard for the loved one, giving and receiving of emotional support, and being able to count on the loved one in times of need.

Passion

Passion refers to the drives that contribute to romance, physical attraction, and sexual consummation in loving relationships (Sternberg, 1986). It is an intense longing for union with the loved one. In a study done on relationship quality among heterosexual dating couples, Fletcher et al. (2000) found that the variable of passion had a positive correlation with relationship quality. The current study looked into the strength of passion and its association with relationship quality. The quantitative results indicated that the majority of the subjects in this sample had a strong sense of passion in their marital relationship. Additionally, the variable of passion had a significant positive correlation with the subjects' relationship quality. The quantitative findings were supported and supplemented by the themes that emerged from the phenomenological interviews. The theme of passion itself captured the subjects' thoughts and feelings about their sense of passion in their relationships. As Sternberg suggested, for several of the subjects, their passionate feelings inevitably interacted with their feelings of intimacy with their spouses.

Although sex and passion were important for the majority of the subjects, a few of them expressed some reservations about giving the dimension of passion undue importance in the overall marital relationship. For example, Khadeejah said, "Our married life is not mainly meant for that [sex]. But it also makes us happy" (Khadeejah, 187–88). The reluctance to give much importance to the dimension of passion in marriage by some of the subjects could be due to cultural factors. As mentioned before, morality regarding sex is a great value in the Indian society (Batabyal, 2001). Premarital sexual relationships and even frequent social interactions between men and women are largely discouraged (D'Cruz and Bharat, 2001; Singh, 2005). Such values and norms of the society might have had some influence on how certain subjects looked at the variable of passion in their marital relationship.

In addition, the Indian society is collectivistic and family-oriented (Chacko, 2003; Chawla, 2007; Jacobson, 1996; Sandhya, 2009). The individual's pleasure is secondary to the well-being of the family. Thus, when it comes to the marital relationship, it is possible that the overall good of the family is given priority over and above the individual's desires and pleasures. However, it should be noted that the majority of the subjects in this study did not consider passion as less important than other variables. Both in quantitative and qualitative responses they expressed that passion was a very important and strongly felt variable in their marital relationships.

Commitment

Commitment consists of a decision to love someone and a commitment to maintain that love (Sternberg, 1986). The current study looked into the strength of commitment and its association with relationship quality in the lives of the participants. Both the quantitative and qualitative results indicated that this sample had a strong sense of commitment in their marital relationship, and commitment was significantly correlated with the subjects' relationship quality. The results indicated that as the level of the subjects' commitment increased, the level of their relationship quality also increased, and vice versa. Themes generated from the phenomenological interviews were consistent with the quantitative findings. The theme of commitment itself reflected the subjects' thoughts and feelings about their sense of commitment in their relationships.

Since faithfulness to one's marital partner and family is considered something like a sacred duty in the Indian culture, it was not surprising to see a high level of commitment in this sample. In addition to the high mean score on commitment in the quantitative responses, the theme of commitment emerged frequently in the interviews. For many of the participants, the themes of commitment, persistence in marriage as a priority, family involvement, and shared values and responsibilities were interrelated. For example, Srinivas felt that certain values that he and his wife held together were the main reason for the strong sense of commitment in their marriage. Most of the subjects indicated that their commitment was not only to their spouses but also to their children and the larger family.

This theme of commitment interacting with family involvement was consistent with the interdependent and collectivistic nature of the Indian society. As Jacobson (1996) and Singh (2005) noted, a marriage in India is a celebration of union, not only of the bride and the groom, but also of two families, two cultures, and/or two religions. The theme of commitment thus applies not only to the couple's relationship but also to the couple's relationship with the extended family and the larger community. It appeared that for this sample, the involvement of the family or community in their marital affairs or their involvement in the affairs of the family or community was a highly regarded value.

Sternberg (1986) had suggested that in arranged marriages, the three components of love—that is, intimacy, passion, and commitment—might be highly imbalanced at the beginning of relationships. He observed that in such marriages, intimacy and passion might be very marginal while commitment might be overemphasized at the beginning of the relationship. Commitment, he noted, could be a generator of intimacy and passion in the course of time. This observation was true for this sample. The majority of the subjects in this sample had a stronger commitment and weaker intimacy and passion at the beginning of their relationships. But gradually the sense of commitment appears to have helped strengthen their intimacy and passion. However, some subjects suggested that the three components of intimacy, passion, and commitment were present from the beginning of their marital relationship. For example, Peter, who was married to his wife only for two years, reported that he and his wife had developed an intimate, passionate, and committed relationship from the very beginning of their relationship. Overall, this sample had a strong sense of commitment and it was a significant contributor to the quality of their marital relationship.

According to the triangular theory of love (Sternberg, 1986), although a perfect match of intimacy, passion, and commitment may be an unrealistic goal, a balanced loving relationship is one in which there is a large amount of love in all the three areas, and all three of them are more or less equally matched. In the current study, the three variables of intimacy, passion, and commitment had high mean scores on their respective scales and all three of them were positively correlated with the subjects' relationship quality. Although it is difficult to discern from these quantitative results whether these three variables were more or less balanced in the subjects' marital relationships, the qualitative results met Sternberg's criteria for evaluating the balance of the three variables and showed that they were more or less balanced in this sample's marital relationships.

Sternberg suggested that one of the ways to assess whether or not the three components are balanced is to take into account how partners express their love in all these three areas. For each of the three variables, Sternberg identified certain "love-action/expression" behaviors. The expression of intimacy, as mentioned before, will consist of partners communicating their inner feelings with each other, promoting each other's well-being, sharing each other's possessions, time, and self, expressing empathy for each other, and offering emotional and material support to each other (Sternberg, 1986). In the current study, the majority of the subjects in the qualitative interviews expressed that their marital relationships were characterized by these expressions of intimacy. For example, Kavya stated that she and her husband had grown to a level of openness and trust in their relationship that she could talk to him about anything. She stated, "Because for me, intimacy is openness. . . . I am so close to him in the sense, I have the openness, or I can talk to him anything in this world" (Kavya, 300–308).

The expression of passion, according to Sternberg (1986), will consist of lovers engaging in kissing, hugging, gazing, touching, and making love. The majority of the subjects in the qualitative phase of the current study expressed that they and their spouses were engaged in various expressions of passion in their marital relationships. For example, Joseph reported, "Certainly, kissing, yes, even the look, you know. That's right. God has, of course, given us wonderful organs like eyes, you know. They are very powerful, and of course, other things automatically follow" (Joseph, 322–24).

The expression of commitment, according to Sternberg (1986), will consist of lovers pledging their commitment and fidelity to each other, staying in the relationship through hard times, and deciding to get engaged and married. The subjects in the current study, specifically, in the qualitative interviews, described how they and their partners expressed their commitment to each other. For example, Priya expressed her commitment to her spouse through a willingness to make any sacrifice for the sake of the relationship. She said, "I am ready to sacrifice anything for this relationship" (Priya, 217–18).

Thus, based on Sternberg's (1986) criteria of "love-action/expression behaviors" for evaluating the balance among the three variables of intimacy, passion, and commitment, and taking into account such expressions of love in this sample, it can be stated that these three variables were more or less balanced in their marital relationships.

In descriptions of relationship quality and variables contributing to relationship quality, various authors have stated that healthy and happy marriages are those that are characterized by a sense of satisfaction, intimacy, mutual understanding, investments, acceptance and adjustments, commitment, developing common goals and values, and satisfactory emotional and sexual relationship (Allendorf and Ghimire, 2013; Bradbury et al., 2000; Gottman and Gottman, 2008). The discussions above looked at the results of the current study, both in its quantitative and qualitative formats, and found that these variables that are associated with healthy and happy marriages are present in this sample. The mean scores, the correlation results, and the multiple linear regression results from the quantitative phase of the study as discussed above present a very positive and healthy picture of the state of marital relationship in this sample. These results were consistent with the results from the qualitative data. The themes generated from the phenomenological interviews supported the quantitative findings and presented a positive picture of the marital relationship in this sample.

Although some of the past studies might give an impression that Indian arranged marriages are unhappy, the current study, both in its quantitative and qualitative formats, indicated that many of the features that are usually associated with healthy and happy marriages were found in this sample. The themes of satisfaction, investments, intimacy, passion, commitment, little instances of love, persistence, and acceptance and understanding were valuable findings about the state of marital relationships in this sample. The subjects indicated that their marital relationships were characterized by mutual understanding, acceptance, adjustments, and common goals and values. They reported that they had a satisfactory emotional and sexual relationship. All of them stated that persistence in their marriages was a priority. All these findings, by and large, point to the conclusion that this sample has a healthy and happy feeling about their marital relationships.

Gender Difference

The current study had hypothesized that there would be differences between men and women in their description of relationship quality, satisfaction, quality of alternatives, investments, intimacy, passion, and commitment. However, the results did not show a significant difference between men and women in their response to any of the measures.

These results were very different from the findings in the studies done in the past on marriages of choice and other romantic relationships. The study done by Rusbult et al. (1998) showed a gender difference with regard to satisfaction, quality of alternatives, investments, and commitment. In comparison to men, women had higher satisfaction, fewer alternatives, greater investment, and stronger commitment. Likewise, Rhyne's (1981) study on marital satisfaction among married Canadians showed that men were generally more satisfied with their marriage than women. But the quantitative findings from the current study did not show any such gender difference for any of the variables.

No conclusive statements about gender difference on any of these variables could be drawn from the qualitative results or themes of the current study, as no specific themes regarding this matter emerged from the phenomenological interviews.

However, although it is not a significant difference, looking at both the quantitative and qualitative data results, one cannot but notice that when it comes to commitment in marriage, there is a slight difference in mean scores between men and women that did not reach statistical significance. In the mean scores of both genders for commitment, the women had a slightly higher mean score than men. For all the other variables, men had a slightly higher mean score. Again, it is difficult to discern from the qualitative interviews if there was a difference between men and women regarding commitment. The only exception in the qualitative interviews regarding this variable was the response of Mary, one of the subjects, who reported that she had an unhappy marriage and yet remained very committed to her spouse. She reported that her husband was her first priority when it came to commitments in her life. She stated, "I used to tell him always, 'I still love you very much, because you are the one person who chose me.' So if he beats me also, no problem, I am happy. I don't want to leave him" (Mary, 338–43).

Although Mary's response does not point to any significant difference in commitment between men and women in this sample, it is important to see her response in the context of the cultural expectations of Indian women in general. The existing literature suggested that women were expected to play many roles in a family (e.g., Chawla, 2006; Khalakdina, 2008; Singh, 2005; Vanita, 2003). She has to be a mother, efficient housekeeper, and obedient and submissive wife and daughter-in-law. These expectations and responsibilities could automatically gear women toward a stronger commitment to their families and fidelity to their spouses.

The absence of any significant gender difference on any of the variables in the quantitative data could be because of the specific characteristics of this sample. The sample in the current study came from an urban and educated section of the society. The majority of them were employed, with about 60 percent of them being teachers and 70 percent of them belonging to the high income group. All of them came from urban settings. In this sample, gender difference may be relatively absent because of the gender equality the subjects maintain in their spousal relationships. Studies have shown that there is greater gender equality in urban areas, and that, in turn, positively influences marital and family relationships (e.g., Mishra et al., 2014; Zuo, 2013).

Studies done on gender and power also have shown that gender difference tends to disappear when performance expectations (e.g., task-related behaviors) for men and women are more or less equalized, and when women are empowered (providing education, reducing job discrimination, reducing violence against women, balancing unequal obligations, and changing discriminatory cultural ideologies (Ridgeway and Bourg, 2004; Pratto and Walker, 2004). Although no specific themes regarding gender equality emerged from the phenomenological interviews, the researcher felt that the women in this sample belonged to the "empowered" group in the society, and that may indicate relatively greater gender equality in their relationship settings. Thus, the characteristics such as education, high income, and urban setting might be contributing to better gender equality among this sample, and that, in turn, might have influenced the description of their marital relationship. As some studies (e.g., Zhang et al., 2007) point out, descriptions of marital and family relationships may be different if the sample came from a rural setting, low-income group, uneducated population, or other settings.

Additionally, the responses from the subjects in the qualitative interviews, particularly those connected with the themes of the essential elements for success in marriage and assessment of marital relationship, point to the cultural imperative that both partners have to put a lot of effort into being relatively high in satisfaction, investments, intimacy, passion, and commitment, and relatively low in alternatives in order to make their marriages work. Further, as mentioned above, families finalize marital alliances only after both parties meet each other's most important demands and expectations. Such cultural imperatives and expectations could be instrumental in minimizing or eliminating gender difference.

Additional Themes from the Interviews

The qualitative interviews generated two themes that were not measured by the quantitative measures. They are: *limited premarital contact* and *religion and spirituality*. It was felt important to discuss these themes as they appeared significant for this sample in the assessment of their marital relationships.

Limited Premarital Contact

All the subjects reported that they had very limited knowledge about their spouses before their marriage. Their interactions were brief and sketchy. They shared that even though they met their prospective spouses once or twice prior to their marriage, the meetings were often held in the presence of other family members, and the conversations were very brief. They reported that sometimes interactions were as brief as ten minutes. For example, Arpitha reported that she and her husband were total strangers before marriage. She stated, "Actually I never saw him before, absolutely strangers" (Arpitha, 27–29).

This theme was consistent with the existing literature on mate selection and marital practices in arranged marriages in India. Being collectivistic, hierarchical, and caste-ridden, the Indian society places many prohibitions and restrictions on cross-gender interactions (Alexander et al., 2006; Batabyal, 2001; Chawla, 2007; Myers et al., 2005; Philips, 2004; Singh, 2005). The society does not approve of open interactions or relationships between the two genders outside of marriage. There are many restrictions about boys and girls or men and women mingling with each other outside of their marital or family circle. Hence, prospective brides and grooms have very limited knowledge of each other prior to their marriage. In this context, children often count on the wisdom and experience of the parents and responsible adults in the family to guide them in choosing their partners. Although the subjects in the current study did not see it as a major problem, this theme of limited knowledge and interactions before marriage was reflected in their responses during the interviews.

Although this theme does not directly contribute to the growth or development of relationship quality, it indicates how and where couples in arranged marriages in India begin their marital relationship. Most of them begin as total strangers. But they gradually move into solidifying their relationships and living healthy and happy marriages. To discuss it further, studies have shown that many marriages of choice and romantic relationships are highly satisfying and positive (e.g., Gottman and Gottman, 2008). Some studies have shown that marriages of choice have even higher satisfaction than arranged marriages (e.g., Xiaohe and Whyte, 1990). Given this context, the findings of the current study were very significant. Despite the fact that all the subjects in this sample had very little premarital contact, both the quantitative and qualitative results revealed that these traditional arranged marriages in India also were high quality relationships with many positive characteristics. The majority of the subjects, both in their quantitative and qualitative responses, indicated that their marriages were marked by a sense of high satisfaction, high intimacy, high passion, high commitment, and high investments.

Religion and Spirituality

The theme of the importance of religion and spirituality in family life and marital relationships emerged from many of the interviews. This theme was not assessed by the quantitative measures. The participants indicated that their religious beliefs were an important factor in strengthening their marital bond and family life. For example, Peter stated that he and his wife were very religious, and their religious practices were helpful in building up their relationship. He reported: "On every Saturday we pray the rosary together. Yes, it is very important. Religion, like, it's my family background. Everyone is very religious and that is my background. I also believe in all that" (Peter, 161–66).

This theme of religion and spirituality was related to another theme in this study, shared values and responsibilities. Religion and spirituality came under the umbrella of shared values that facilitated and promoted the subjects' relationship quality. The subjects indicated that common interests with regard to religion and spirituality helped them to make their marital relationships healthy and happy.

This theme of religion and spirituality was consistent with the existing literature on the role of religion and spirituality in Indian marriages. Religion plays a major role in marital and family life in India. Several authors, including Bose and South (2003), Chawla (2007), Chekki (1996), and Singh (2005), noted that Indians, in general, and Hindus, in particular, believed in the inevitability of marriage. This belief, the authors said, is derived mostly from religious texts such as *Vedas*, *Smrithis*, and *Upanishads*, which considered marriage as a duty and sacrament that was required of all human beings. Stipulations about how to live one's marital and family life are also contained in these religious texts and teachings (Chawla, 2007). Although the subjects in the current study came from different religious backgrounds, religion and spirituality appeared to be a very significant factor for all of them in their marital decisions and relationships.

14

Interpretation of the Findings

HAVING LOOKED AT THE overall findings and discussed the correspondence between the quantitative and the qualitative results of this study, the following sections will present observations, reflections, and interpretations on the findings of this study, and show how they relate to the existing literature.

HIGHER FUNCTIONING RELATIONSHIPS

The results of this study showed that the subjects in this sample had developed their marriages into higher functioning relationships. As mentioned above, for the general question on the quality of marital relationship, 98 percent of the subjects rated the overall quality of their marital relationship as positive. These findings put this sample at a higher percentage of relationship quality than those found in some of the past studies done on marriages of choice and even arranged marriages.

In line with what the investment model suggests, the majority of the participants in the current study were greatly satisfied, highly invested, and found their best match in their marital partners. The sample had also obtained a large amount of love and a good balance of the three components of love in their marital relationships as the triangular theory of love suggested. The high mean scores for the variables of intimacy, passion, and commitment indicated that they had a large amount of love in these three areas of their relationships. The various expressions of intimacy, passion, and commitment, as described by the subjects in the qualitative interviews, confirmed that they had obtained a good balance of these three components of love.

The attainment of a large amount of love and a good balance of the three ingredients of love, according to Sternberg (1986), point to a complete or consummate love. The subjects of the current study thus appeared to have developed such a love relationship in their marriages. Couples who develop such love relationships, according to Gottman and Gottman (2008), belong to a category called "masters of relationship." The subjects in this sample, therefore, could be called "masters of relationship." They reported in both the qualitative and quantitative formats that their relationships were stable and that they felt relatively happy in their marriages across time.

TRANSITION FROM STRANGERS TO SPOUSES

The results showed that the subjects in this sample had made a transition from being consenters to an arranged relationship to becoming partners in a happy marital relationship. In other words, as the title of this study indicates, they had moved from being "strangers" to becoming "spouses" in a happy relationship. This transition from being strangers to spouses was described more in the responses of the individuals who participated in the qualitative interviews.

Some of the subjects described that it didn't take too long to make this transition. For example, Renuka said, "Actually for us it was not that difficult, because somehow, we both are [have] same behavior and same type of likings" (Renuka, 40–41). But for the majority of the subjects, the movement from being strangers to becoming happy couples was a gradual process. The response of one of the participants, Arpitha, illustrates this point.

Arpitha and her husband appeared to have gone through what the ecological systems theorists called the different stages of dyadic development—that is, they moved through a transition from being an observational dyad to becoming a primary dyad by growing in their affective feelings for each other and influencing each other's behavior (Bronfenbrenner, 1979). Arpitha reported that she and her husband began their marital life as strangers. "Actually I never saw him before, absolutely strangers" (Arpitha, 27–28). Then it took them a few years to understand and connect with each other. She stated, "I think it took three to four years by the time he started understanding me" (Arpitha, 55–56). And now after completing twelve years of marriage, she felt that they had become a happy couple, a primary dyad. She said, "Pretty happy, on top of the world. And completely satisfied" (Arpitha, 61).

The responses of Priya and Peter were similar in nature. Priya stated, "We are almost like friends, more than husband and wife. Very happy with my relationship" (Priya, 57–58). Peter's response was, "Still we are like friends. . . . She sometimes calls me as if my friend is calling, by name, like friends call, with friends' initials and all that" (Peter, 186–89). Like these three subjects, Arpitha, Priya, and Peter, the majority of the respondents in the qualitative phase of the study reported that they had made that transition from being strangers to becoming happy spouses gradually. Over the course of time, they were able to solidify their relationship by developing what the attachment theorists called a strong and secure attachment bond (Bowlby, 1988; Hughes, 2004, 2007, 2009; Sayre et al., 2010).

This gradual process of transitioning from being strangers to becoming spouses appears to be a characteristic specific to arranged marriages and collectivistic cultures. In collectivistic cultures, where arranged marriages are the predominant form of marriage, people get married first and then work toward developing their relationships into intimate friendships. Such a take on marriages and spousal relationships may be somewhat startling for people in individualistic cultures and marriages of choice. In marriages of choice or love marriages, as discussed before, two individuals develop a relationship of familiarity and friendship before they enter into a marital commitment. They would expect intimacy and love to precede their marriage rather than expecting them to happen after marriage. Ordinarily, they would not think that two people could enter into a marital relationship without being friends first. But the participants in the current study appear to suggest that such arrangements and relationship dynamics are possible and even successful.

The current study also appears to be suggesting that these differences in perspectives and practices need to be seen from the context of the differences between individualistic and collectivistic cultures. While for those in individualistic cultures and marriages of choice, building a loving and intimate relationship with one's partner precedes marriage, for those in collectivistic cultures and arranged marriages, it is a post-marital task. The study suggested that even though the subjects in this sample began their marital lives with limited knowledge about each other and minimal love and intimacy, they were able to take their relationships to higher levels of growth. They transitioned into being satisfied, intimate, passionate, committed, and highly invested couples.

PERSISTENCE IN MARRIAGE

Another notable feature of this sample was that persistence in marriage was a priority for all of them. As noted before, faithfulness and commitment to one's marital partner are highly valued concepts in the Indian culture. These culturally embedded themes were reflected in the qualitative responses of the participants. The participants indicated strong reservation on their part to think of anything or anybody in the place of their spouses. For example, one of the subjects, Mary, who had a difficult and unhappy marriage, indicated that when it came to commitment and persistence in marriage, she would not allow anything to sabotage her marriage or minimize her commitment to her spouse. She said, "I used to tell him always, 'whatever you do to me, I still love you very much, because you are the one person who chose me' . . . If he beats me also, no problem, I don't want to leave him" (Mary, 338–43). When asked what made her stay married in such an abusive relationship, Mary said, "It is because of the marriage vows. I have given myself to him, and I have promised to love him no matter what" (Mary, 359–60).

Several authors, such as Chacko (2003) and Singh (2005), had reported the presence of widespread violence and abuses in many Indian marriages. Interestingly, Singh (2005) had reported that three out of five Indian women believed that wife beating was justified. Women accepted the right of husbands to use force to discipline them. Mary's response appeared to indicate that the cultural expectations regarding commitment and persistence in marriage made her tolerate her abuses and negative experiences. However, it is to be noted that neither the quantitative measures nor the qualitative interviews in this study assessed the variable of violence in this sample. The response of Mary was more in relation to the variable of commitment than violence. Hence, based on the scope and results of this study, it is difficult to make any statement about how the description of the relationship quality in this sample would have been if the variable of violence also were assessed. Given the context of past studies reporting about the prevalence of high levels of violence in such marriages, one of the limitations of this study was the absence of any assessment of violence in this sample.

COLLECTIVISM AND INTERDEPENDENCE

This study showed that collectivism and interdependence were integral ingredients of marital relationships of this sample. As several authors have noted, collectivism and interdependence are celebrated features of the Indian society and family system (Hoelter et al., 2004; Jacobson, 1996; Joshi, 2010; Medora, 2007). Marriages in India are not just between two individuals but rather two families, two communities, and sometimes even two cultures. When two people get married in India, particularly in the tradition of arranged marriages, there is a celebrated meeting of traditional values, kinship bond, social and familial obligations, and impassioned sentiments (Jacobson, 1996). The presence of these features of collectivism and interdependence in this sample's marital relationships and relationship quality was reflected in all the themes, but particularly in the themes of family involvement and assessment of marital relationship. The responses of all the participants in the qualitative interviews indicated that their families actively participated in matters concerning their marriage, both before and after their marriage. Most of these participants who were interviewed found the involvement of the family as a blessing in their lives, and it appeared to improve the quality of their marital relationships.

The features of collectivism and interdependence were seen in the sample's overall assessment of marital relationship. Looking at the responses of the interview participants, the researcher learned that when it came to an evaluation of their marriage and marital relationship, the subjects looked at them through the lens of collectivism and interdependence rather than individualism. In their mind, when it comes to the overall evaluation of their life or marriage, it is not just about them or their individual satisfaction. What is most important for them is the good of the family. And the good of the family might mean honoring the sacredness of the marriage, honoring the marriage vows and being faithful and committed to the spouse, and doing everything for the good of their children. They may have their personal experiences of disappointments and dissatisfaction in marriage, but when it comes to making an overall evaluation of their marriage or marital relationship, they look at what has been good for the family. The respondents appeared to suggest that in order to understand the quality of marital relationship in arranged marriages in India it was important to understand the value of family ties and cultural expectations.

This way of looking at their relationship quality through the lens of collectivism and interdependence was illustrated in the responses of one of the subjects, Jaya, for example. Jaya, a sixty-six-year-old woman, who was married to her husband for forty-nine years, indicated during the interview that she had many disappointments in her marriage, but when it came to assessing her marital relationship, the overall good of her family seemed to be the most important determining factor. Here are some examples of her responses to this effect. She said that she had consistently longed for some affection from her husband but never received it. "He is something, very rough, rough person. And also, I expect so many times that he talks to me very affectionately, very close, so many times. But that is not his nature" (Jaya, 241–42). She and her husband had not had any physical or sexual relationship for a long time and they didn't sleep together anymore. "We have not had sex for almost fifteen years. . . . Both of us are not sleeping together" (Jaya, 272, 320). She reported that she liked to talk to him but he did not like to do it. "So, actually, he does not want to express, open, he does not want to talk. I like to talk, but he does not want to talk" (Jaya, 328–29). She reported that she did not go anywhere leaving him alone, but there is no reciprocity from his side. "Even though he goes outside [away] for many days, but I don't like to leave him alone at home. He leaves" (Jaya, 380–85). She stated that her husband made most of the decisions without consulting her. "He makes those decisions. So many times, I don't like those decisions" (Jaya, 430).

With all these, while describing the overall quality of her marriage, Jaya said, "We are happy. Some problems, misunderstanding, problems, individual problems are there. But we have a strong marriage" (Jaya, 98–99). And her reason for this positive outlook about her marriage was reflected in her comments: "To keep the home and marriage, and everything, to be smooth, and happy, we have to make all these things, all these compromises, should be there. Otherwise, no peace of mind" (Jaya, 263–65).

The responses of Jaya are consistent with what Medora (2007) stated about the condition of many Indian women, that they choose to remain as "silent sufferers" (p. 185) rather than breaking away. Breaking away is perceived to be more painful and shameful for them and their families than staying married and putting up with all the inconveniences. Given this context, it is no surprise that many women are willing to endure violence and abuses for the sake of the good of the family and for their own "peace," as Jaya reported. These responses of Jaya and other female respondents in the study also reflect the condition of women in the Indian society. The current study confirmed what was found in the review of literature regarding the status of women in India. The patriarchal and hierarchical societal system continues to favor men over women when it comes to the decision-making processes and exercise of power in families.

Bronfenbrenner (1979) and others (Chen and Zhang, 2013; McLaren and Hawe, 2005; Neal and Neal, 2013) pointed out that environment was a major factor in determining how easy or difficult it is for couples or individuals to make progress in their personal and dyadic development. The themes and responses of the participants in this study indicated that their culture and environment played a key role in their assessment and description of their relationship quality. Even with all the negative and unsatisfactory experiences they had with their spouses, when it came to the assessment of the quality of their marital relationships, they were not thinking of it just in terms of their personal satisfaction or pleasures alone but rather in the context of the overall picture of their family and community life.

Coontz (2005), in her findings, had reported that for most of human history, the primary focus of marriage was not the accomplishment of individual needs and desires. It was a combination of several things. And that kind of understanding of marriage seemed to be present in this sample of individuals who occupy arranged marriages in India.

The possibility of social desirability bias, a tendency to characterize themselves and their families in a favorable manner, also cannot be ruled out in this study. Sandra Nolte and her colleagues (2013) noted that socially desirable responding is very common in studies that involve telephone and personal interviews. In self-reports, respondents tend to create a positive impression about themselves, their families, and friends, to obtain social approval and avoid disapproval. In the current study, some of the subjects like Jaya, giving a positive picture of the marital relationship despite the many negative experiences, might have been also because of their social desirability bias.

DISSONANCE IN THE LITERATURE

The review of literature in this study had found that there was a dissonance in the current literature about the quality of relationship in arranged marriages in India. Some authors had reported that there was a very high rate of satisfaction or happiness in those marriages while others reported widespread abuse, violence, and discrimination against women in many of those marriages. The subjects in this study looking at the quality of their marital relationship through the lens of collectivism and interdependence rather than individualism might explain to some extent why this dissonance about the quality of relationship in the literature exists.

As stated, all the subjects who participated in the qualitative interviews appeared to suggest that their assessment of their marriages and the description of the relationship quality were dependent on many cultural and familial factors. They looked at the overall good of the family rather than their individual preferences or satisfaction. The response of Jaya, for example, showed that in spite of the many unpleasant and negative experiences she had in her marriage, commitment to her husband and persistence in marriage were high priorities in her life. The subject, Mary, had even acknowledged the presence of violence and abuses in her marriage, but she stated that she was willing to suffer such abuses and personal losses for the sake of the family and commitment to her husband. Similarly, another subject, Priya, reported: "I am ready to sacrifice anything for this relationship" (Priya, 217–18). There were also other subjects who reiterated that their first priority was commitment to their spouses and persistence in marriage rather than their personal satisfaction.

In all of these responses of the participants, what is notable is that in their conceptualization of successful and satisfactory marriages and description of relationship quality, what mattered most was the overall good of their families and marriages rather than their personal preferences and satisfaction. Even though they were subjected to abusive and unpleasant experiences and many of their personal preferences and individual needs remained unfulfilled, they still considered their marriages as successful or high-quality relationships. This way of viewing relationship quality from the perspective of the overall good of the family rather than that of the individual appears to be a characteristic specific to collectivistic cultures.

For people in individualistic cultures and marriages of choice, it may be surprising and even shocking to hear that these individuals in arranged marriages still consider their marriages as high-quality relationships in spite of their experiences of being excluded from the decision-making processes and being subjected to violence and abuses. Ordinarily, no one would expect that domination, violence, and abuses could go hand in hand with happy and satisfactory marriages. In many societies, particularly in individualistic cultures, such negative experiences could be sufficient reason for separation and divorce. But given the fact that for the subjects in the current study the assessment of their marital relationships involved the consideration of many layers of their culture and familial expectations, such negative experiences were not sufficient reason to abandon their marriages or consider them as unsatisfactory. In evaluating their marital relationships, they set aside many of their individual needs and desires and looked at them from the perspective of the overall good of the family.

Medora (2007) had noted that many Indians were influenced by beliefs such as *karma*, which encourages people to accept the inconveniences and difficulties of life uncomplainingly so that they would be rewarded in the next life. When such beliefs are in place, certain individuals might tolerate and even justify the abuses and negative experiences in their marital relationships and continue to think of their marriages as happy and high-quality relationships. The responses of some of the subjects in the current study confirm that their assessment of their marriages was highly influenced by such belief systems and cultural values. As mentioned previously, social desirability bias also could have influenced the responses of the participants. Qualifying their marital relationships as happy and successful even while acknowledging the presence of abuses and violence could be a sign of their desire to present themselves and their families in a favorable manner to the researcher and the outside world.

The dissonance in the existing literature about the quality of relationship might have also been because of the limitations of the methods used in the past studies. One of the limitations of the studies done on arranged marriages in India in the past was that most of them had used a quantitative-only method, which did not fully capture the lived experience of the participants. In that regard, the current study was much more in-depth, providing insights into the lived experiences of a small number of the subjects. If the relationship quality in this sample were looked at only from a quantitative point of view, the findings would have been very limited, because the instruments used in this study look at relationship quality primarily from the perspective of an individual's personal satisfaction. Those instruments are based on marriages of choice and romantic relationships in the West, where the individual's satisfaction is a priority when it comes to the assessment and description of relationship quality.

The instruments developed in the West were useful, and they answered several of the research questions. But they were insufficient to fully understand the research problem in this study. In addition to the quantitative data, it was very beneficial for this study to have a small group of individuals from this sample to participate in qualitative interviews and describe in their own words what they felt about their marital relationships. The themes generated from the qualitative interviews such as commitment, persistence in marriage, and family involvement showed how the cultural elements such as collectivism and interdependence were very important for the subjects in this sample when it came to the assessment and description of their marital relationships. The phenomenological interviews elicited rich responses from the participants about the overall quality of their marital relationships. Hence, the addition of phenomenological interviews helped supplement the quantitative findings and added depth to the understanding of the marital relationships in this sample.

15

Strengths, Limitations, and Recommendations

THIS CHAPTER DISCUSSES THE strengths and limitations of the study and includes recommendations for future research in the area of arranged marriages in India.

STRENGTHS OF THE STUDY

The current study has several strengths. First, the use of mixed methods research helped the researcher to obtain a more comprehensive idea of the relationship quality in this sample of the arranged marriages in India than some of the past studies that were limited in their methodologies. The mixed methods approach did help to address the confirmatory and exploratory research questions of the study simultaneously, and allowed gathering of more in-depth data than a single method would have allowed. Second, based on previous research, the study offered a solid framework to examine and explore relationship quality in this sample of the arranged marriages. All the hypotheses, except one, were confirmed by the results of the study. Third, the study added to the knowledge base already existing about arranged marriages in India. Studies done on arranged marriages in India, particularly mixed methods studies, are still very few in number.

Fourth, the findings of the study are expected to help mental health professionals, particularly marital and family therapists, who treat Indian couples to better understand the specifics of marital relationships in Indian arranged marriages. This will be particularly helpful to clinicians who are unfamiliar with the Indian culture and marital system. Fifth, the study hopefully helped the participants to gain insights about their own marriages. Completing all the questionnaires on the different dimensions of marriage and having an opportunity to share their thoughts and reflections about their personal experience of marriage were hopefully helpful for them to look at their marital relationships afresh and gain some insights.

Sixth, the study is expected to help other Indian couples in arranged marriages to look at the quality of their own marital relationships and learn what it takes to build strong and healthy relationships. It is often helpful and educational to read or listen to what people in similar situations share about their personal experience. Seventh, the phenomenological interviews offered some rich insights into how people in arranged marriages view and experience their marriages and marital relationships. Eighth, the study helped to apply to the Indian population the instruments and theoretical models created in and for the Western society.

LIMITATIONS OF THE STUDY

This study, however, is not without limitations. Although the researcher made an honest effort to remain open and unbiased in the collection, analysis, and interpretation of the data, he cannot guarantee that he was completely free of bias in the study. His background might have had a significant impact on how he gathered, understood, and interpreted the data. He is also aware that when people were being interviewed and observed, it might have made them uneasy. When he was interviewing them, he was in fact entering into their "personal territory," and it is possible that they acted and responded differently from what they would normally have done in an ordinary conversation with someone.

Since one of the criteria for being a participant in the study was to be able to speak and understand English, the study automatically kept out of its purview all other Indians who do not speak and understand English. Indians who speak and understand English are largely the educated and urbanized population of the country, and all the participants of the current study were educated, with 92 percent of them having a bachelor's or a higher degree. Hence, the participants of the present study do not represent the uneducated and rural population of the nation. Although the researcher hoped to recruit an equal number of participants from both genders, the number of men who participated in the study was low. For the quantitative phase, 76.7 percent of the participants were women, and only 23.3 percent were men. For the qualitative phase, 64.3 percent of the participants were women, and 35.7 percent were men.

Another limitation of this study is the failure to assess and solicit data pertaining to violence and power in this sample. Neither the quantitative measures nor the qualitative interviews in this study assessed the variable of violence in this sample. Since some past studies had indicated that there was a high level of violence, particularly against women in many arranged marriages in India, it would have been very useful to get the subjects' responses on the level of violence and perceptions of violence against women in this sample. Such data would have provided additional clarification regarding the relationship between reports of high satisfaction and high levels of violence against women in such marriages.

Although the quantitative phase of the study had a relatively large sample, the limitation of not having a random sample and doing the parametric tests with a convenience sample might have affected the accuracy of the findings. Finally, although the researcher obtained rich data on the relationship quality in this sample of arranged marriages, a larger sample with more diversity might produce better data on the relationship quality in arranged marriages in India.

GENERALIZABILITY AND RECOMMENDATIONS

Quantitative researchers talk of the generalizability of their study findings and qualitative researchers often refer to the same through the concept of transferability. The question is whether the findings of the current study can be generalized or transferred to all arranged marriages in India or elsewhere. As mentioned before, Sandhya (2009) pointed out that generalization of research findings in the Indian context is questionable due to the regional differences in family, language, caste, class, religion, customs, and traditions. The findings and narratives in the current study are not representative of the experience of all Indians in arranged marriages, and hence the findings do not represent all arranged marriages in India. Additionally, this study had a small sample size, particularly for the qualitative interviews. Hence, this sample does not represent all Indians or all arranged marriages in India. However, the possibilities of generalization cannot be completely ruled out because there are "some striking generalities" (Sandhya, 2009, p. 92) in the family and marital system across India. Although the current study focused more on its exploratory value than its generalizability, its applicability to marital relationships in the Indian context in general cannot be discounted.

To get a wider perspective of the relationship quality in the arranged marriages in India, it is recommended that this study be extended to a larger population, with an even larger sample. That would include taking samples from rural settings, the non-English speaking population, and people from several more states, regions, religions, and other groups in the Indian society. Another direction for future research is a mixed methods study comparing the relationship quality in arranged marriages and marriages of choice in India. Building on that, a similar mixed methods study could be done comparing the relationship quality in arranged marriages in India and marriages of choice in an individualistic culture, such as the United States. Future studies could also assess relationship quality and the presence of violence together to get additional clarification regarding the relationship between reports of high quality and high levels of violence against women in arranged marriages in India.

Conclusion

ARRANGED MARRIAGES IN INDIA has been a fascinating topic of study for many researchers. This particular mixed methods study explored the relationship quality in those marriages. Specifically, it looked into the level of marital satisfaction, quality of alternatives, investment of resources, intimacy, passion, and commitment in arranged marriages in India, and examined their association with relationship quality. The survey was composed of seven measures, and the qualitative interviews consisted of phenomenological interviews with the researcher. The survey was completed by 287 participants, and 14 of these respondents completed qualitative interviews.

Both the quantitative and qualitative data generated rich results with regard to the relationship quality in this sample. Both data sets supported the main hypotheses of the study regarding relationship quality. The results of the quantitative data showed that there was a high level of relationship quality, satisfaction, investments, intimacy, passion, and commitment and a low level of quality of alternatives in this sample. All the six independent variables were significantly correlated with relationship quality. The multiple linear regression also was found to be statistically significant. The results showed no significant difference between men and women for any of the variables.

The qualitative findings were consistent with the quantitative results. Five major themes were generated from the qualitative data: family involvement, limited premarital contact, essential elements for success, assessment of marital relationship, and persistence in marriage as a priority. Some of these themes had sub-themes to follow. Quotes and comments from the participants were cited to validate the accuracy of the themes.

The combination of both the quantitative and qualitative data was found to be very beneficial in eliciting rich responses from the subjects and evaluating the relationship quality in their marriages. Although the measures used in the survey were developed in the West based on studies of romantic relationships or marriages of choice, they were useful and applicable in the Indian context of arranged marriages. The phenomenological interviews helped supplement the quantitative data and provided rich insights into the lived experience of a small number of the subjects.

The findings of the study add to the existing literature on arranged marriages in India. Reading this book, some people might wonder whether arranged marriages are better than marriages of choice or vice versa. The focus of this study was not any such comparison between arranged marriages and marriages of choice or between collectivistic cultures and individualistic cultures. Every culture is unique, and so is every type of marriage. This study specifically looked at arranged marriages in the particular context of India. The results presented here give a good sense of how couples in this type of marriage in India view and assess their marital relationships. It is hoped that these findings would help couples and clinicians to better understand the personal, familial, and cultural specificities of this universal institution of marriage in the particular context of India.

Appendix A

Demographic Information

PLEASE CHECK, CIRCLE, OR fill in your responses for the following:

1. Your Gender: _____ Male _____ Female

2. Your Age: _____

3. Your Religion:

Christian   Hindu   Muslim   Other (specify) _____

4. Number of years married to your current partner _____

5. Are you employed?   Yes   No

6. If you are employed, what is your occupation/Job? _____

7. How would you rate the economic status of your family in terms of annual income?

| Less than Rs. 25,000 | Rs. 26,000– 50,000 | Rs. 50,000+ |

8. Your level of education:

| Did not complete High School | Completed High School | Bachelors Degree or higher |

Appendix B

Relationship Assessment Scale

FOR THE FOLLOWING ITEMS indicate the degree to which you are satisfied with your relationship with your husband/wife.

How well does your partner meet your needs?	1 Poorly	2	3 Average	4	5 Extremely well
In general, how satisfied are you with your relationship?	1 Unsatisfied	2	3 Average	4	5 Extremely satisfied
How good is your relationship compared to most?	1 Poor	2	3 Average	4	5 Excellent
How often do you wish you hadn't gotten into this relationship?	1 Never	2	3 Average	4	5 Very often
To what extent has your relationship met your original expectations?	1 Hardly at all	2	3 Average	4	5 Completely
How much do you love your partner?	1 Not much	2	3 Average	4	5 Very much
How many problems are there in your relationship?	1 Very few	2	3 Average	4	5 Very many

Appendix C

Investment Model Scale

PLEASE INDICATE THE DEGREE to which you agree with each of the following statements regarding your current marital relationship. Please circle an answer or number for each item.

Satisfaction				
My partner fulfills my needs for intimacy (sharing personal thoughts, secrets, etc.)	Don't agree at all	Agree Slightly	Agree Moderately	Agree Completely
My partner fulfills my needs for companionship (doing things together, enjoying each other's company, etc.)	Don't agree at all	Agree Slightly	Agree Moderately	Agree Completely
My partner fulfills my sexual needs (holding hands, kissing, etc.)	Don't agree at all	Agree Slightly	Agree Moderately	Agree Completely
My partner fulfills my needs for security (feeling trusting, comfortable in a stable relationship, etc.)	Don't agree at all	Agree Slightly	Agree Moderately	Agree Completely
My partner fulfills my needs for emotional involvement (feeling emotionally attached, feeling good when another feels good, etc.)	Don't agree at all	Agree Slightly	Agree Moderately	Agree Completely

	Do not agree at all				Agree Moderately				Agree Completely
I feel satisfied with our relationship	1	2	3	4	5	6	7	8	9
My relationship is much better than others' relationships	1	2	3	4	5	6	7	8	9
My relationship is close to ideal.	1	2	3	4	5	6	7	8	9
Our relationship makes me very happy.	1	2	3	4	5	6	7	8	9
Our relationship does a good job of fulfilling my needs for intimacy, companionship, etc.	1	2	3	4	5	6	7	8	9

Please indicate the degree to which you agree with each statement regarding the fulfillment of each need in alternative relationships (e.g., by another marital partner, friends, family). Please circle an answer or number for each item.

Quality of Alternatives				
My needs for intimacy (sharing personal thoughts, secrets, etc.) could be fulfilled in alternative relationships.	Don't agree at all	Agree Slightly	Agree Moderately	Agree Completely
My needs for companionship (doing things together, enjoying each other's company, etc.) could be fulfilled in alternative relationships	Don't agree at all	Agree Slightly	Agree Moderately	Agree Completely
My sexual needs (holding hands, kissing, etc.) could be fulfilled in alternative relationships.	Don't agree at all	Agree Slightly	Agree Moderately	Agree Completely
My needs for security (feeling trusting, comfortable in a stable relationship, etc.) could be fulfilled in alternative relationships.	Don't agree at all	Agree Slightly	Agree Moderately	Agree Completely
My needs for emotional involvement (feeling emotionally attached, feeling good when another feels good, etc.) could be fulfilled in alternative relationships.	Don't agree at all	Agree Slightly	Agree Moderately	Agree Completely

	Do not agree at all				Agree Moderately			Agree Completely
The people other than my partner with whom I might become involved are very appealing.	1	2	3	4	5	6	7	8	9
My alternatives to our relationship are close to ideal (marrying another, spending time with friends or on my own, etc.)	1	2	3	4	5	6	7	8	9
If I weren't married to my partner, I would do fine—I would find another appealing person to marry.	1	2	3	4	5	6	7	8	9
My alternatives are attractive to me (marrying another, spending time with friends or on my own).	1	2	3	4	5	6	7	8	9
My needs for intimacy, companionship, etc., could easily be fulfilled in an alternative relationship.	1	2	3	4	5	6	7	8	9

Please indicate the degree to which you agree with each of the following statements regarding your current marital relationship. Please circle an answer or number for each item.

Investment Size				
I have invested a great deal of time in our relationship	Don't agree at all	Agree Slightly	Agree Moderately	Agree Completely
I have told my partner many private things about myself (I disclose secrets to him/her)	Don't agree at all	Agree Slightly	Agree Moderately	Agree Completely
My partner and I have an intellectual life together that would be difficult to replace	Don't agree at all	Agree Slightly	Agree Moderately	Agree Completely
My sense of personal identity (who I am) is linked to my partner and our relationship	Don't agree at all	Agree Slightly	Agree Moderately	Agree Completely
My partner and I share many memories	Don't agree at all	Agree Slightly	Agree Moderately	Agree Completely

	Do not agree at all				Agree Moderately			Agree Completely
I have put a great deal into our relationship that I would lose if the relationship were to end.	1	2	3	4	5	6	7	8	9
Many aspects of my life have become linked to my partner (recreational activities, etc.), and I would lose all of this if I were to break up.	1	2	3	4	5	6	7	8	9
I feel very involved in our relationship—like I have put a great deal into it.	1	2	3	4	5	6	7	8	9
My relationships with friends and family members would be complicated if my partner and I were to break up (e.g., partner is friends with people I care about).	1	2	3	4	5	6	7	8	9
Compared to other people I know, I have invested a great deal in my relationship with my partner.	1	2	3	4	5	6	7	8	9

Appendix D

Triangular Love Scale

PLEASE CIRCLE A NUMBER for each of the following statements that best describes your relationship with your husband/wife.

Intimacy	Not at all				Moderately				Extremely
I am actively supportive of my partner's well-being.	1	2	3	4	5	6	7	8	9
I have a warm relationship with my partner.	1	2	3	4	5	6	7	8	9
I am able to count on my partner in times of need.	1	2	3	4	5	6	7	8	9
My partner is able to count on me in times of need.	1	2	3	4	5	6	7	8	9
I am willing to share myself and my possessions with my partner.	1	2	3	4	5	6	7	8	9
I receive considerable emotional support from my partner.	1	2	3	4	5	6	7	8	9

Intimacy	Not at all				Moderately				Extremely
I give considerable emotional support to my partner.	1	2	3	4	5	6	7	8	9
I communicate well with my partner.	1	2	3	4	5	6	7	8	9
I value my partner greatly in my life.	1	2	3	4	5	6	7	8	9
I feel close to my partner.	1	2	3	4	5	6	7	8	9
I have a comfortable relationship with my partner	1	2	3	4	5	6	7	8	9
I feel that I really understand my partner	1	2	3	4	5	6	7	8	9
I feel that my partner really understands me	1	2	3	4	5	6	7	8	9
I feel that I can really trust my partner	1	2	3	4	5	6	7	8	9
I share deeply personal information about myself with my partner	1	2	3	4	5	6	7	8	9

Passion	Not at all				Moderately				Extremely
Just seeing my partner excites me	1	2	3	4	5	6	7	8	9
I find myself thinking about my partner frequently during the day	1	2	3	4	5	6	7	8	9
My relationship with my partner is very romantic	1	2	3	4	5	6	7	8	9

Passion	Not at all				Moderately				Extremely
I find my partner to be very personally attractive	1	2	3	4	5	6	7	8	9
I idealize my partner	1	2	3	4	5	6	7	8	9
I cannot imagine another person making me as happy as my partner does	1	2	3	4	5	6	7	8	9
I would rather be with my partner than with anyone else	1	2	3	4	5	6	7	8	9
There is nothing more important to me than my relationship with my partner	1	2	3	4	5	6	7	8	9
I especially like physical contact with my partner	1	2	3	4	5	6	7	8	9
There is something almost "magical" about my relationship with my partner	1	2	3	4	5	6	7	8	9
I adore my partner	1	2	3	4	5	6	7	8	9
I cannot imagine life without my partner	1	2	3	4	5	6	7	8	9
My relationship with my partner is passionate	1	2	3	4	5	6	7	8	9
When I see romantic movies or read romantic books I think of my partner	1	2	3	4	5	6	7	8	9
I fantasize about my partner	1	2	3	4	5	6	7	8	9

Commitment	Not at all				Moderately				Extremely
I know that I care about my partner	1	2	3	4	5	6	7	8	9
I am committed to maintaining my relationship with my partner	1	2	3	4	5	6	7	8	9
Because of my commitment to my partner, I would not let other people come between us	1	2	3	4	5	6	7	8	9
I have confidence in the stability of my relationship with my partner	1	2	3	4	5	6	7	8	9
I could not let anything get in the way of my commitment to my partner	1	2	3	4	5	6	7	8	9
I expect my love for my partner to last for the rest of my life	1	2	3	4	5	6	7	8	9
I will always have a strong responsibility for my partner	1	2	3	4	5	6	7	8	9
I view my commitment to my partner as a solid one	1	2	3	4	5	6	7	8	9
I cannot imagine ending my relationship with my partner	1	2	3	4	5	6	7	8	9
I am certain of my love for my partner	1	2	3	4	5	6	7	8	9
I view my relationship with my partner as permanent	1	2	3	4	5	6	7	8	9

Commitment	Not at all				Moderately				Extremely
I view my relationship with my partner as a good decision	1	2	3	4	5	6	7	8	9
I feel a sense of responsibility toward my partner	1	2	3	4	5	6	7	8	9
I plan to continue in my relationship with my partner	1	2	3	4	5	6	7	8	9
Even when my partner is hard to deal with, I remain committed to our relationship	1	2	3	4	5	6	7	8	9

Appendix E

General Question on the Overall Relationship Quality

1. How would you rate the overall quality of your relationship with your husband/wife?

   ☐ Positive   ☐ Negative

Appendix F

Qualitative Phase Interview Guide

BEFORE THE INTERVIEWS BEGAN, I reviewed the purpose and procedures of the research study, emphasized the voluntary nature of the study, reviewed how I would maintain confidentiality, and obtained the subjects' verbal consent.

There are no right or wrong answers to this; all married persons are different. I am a student researcher, and I am interested in your experiences as an individual living in an arranged marriage. Thank you for allowing me to be here (Sample of Introduction).

SEMI-STRUCTURED QUESTIONS

1. Could you tell me a little bit about your marriage?
    a. When and how did you get married?
    b. Who was involved in arranging it?
    c. What was the measure of your participation in making the decision?

2. As much as possible, describe in your own words the overall feeling you have about your marital relationship now.
    a. Are you happy and satisfied in this relationship?
    b. How healthy is your relationship with your spouse?
    c. What is and what is not helpful in making your marriage happy and successful?
    d. In your opinion, what makes a marriage happy and successful?

3. Could you tell me a little bit about the level of support you receive in your marriage?
   a. What are the things that have a positive and negative impact on your marital relationship?
   b. What would you say is the level of support you are receiving from your spouse?
   c. Do you think you and your spouse are pretty committed in this relationship?
   d. What kind of support system do you have in terms of family or community?
   e. In an ideal situation, what would make you feel that you are supported?

4. How close and intimate do you feel to your spouse?
   a. How would you describe the level of closeness, sense of warmth, affection, and emotional connection you feel with your spouse?
   b. Any pleasant memories that stand out to you?
   c. In your thinking, what would make a relationship intimate?

5. How comfortable do you feel in disclosing to your spouse your personal and private thoughts and feelings?
   a. If and when you disclose your private thoughts and feelings, how does your spouse respond?
   b. Would you consider your spouse like a friend?

6. Could you tell me about your physical and sexual relationship with your spouse?
   a. The physical expressions of your love like kissing, hugging, touching?
   b. Sexual expressions like how often you have sex, who initiates sex, and how satisfied you are about your sexual relationship?

7. What makes you stay married to your spouse?
   a. Do you think your marriage fulfills your most important needs?
   b. How would you rate the availability of other alternatives to fulfill your most important needs?

8. How much do you think you have invested in this relationship?
   a. How does that impact your relationship with your spouse?
   b. What would happen if this relationship were to end?

9. Is there anything else that you would like to tell me about your marital relationship?

Bibliography

Adams, Bert N., and Jan Trost. "Epilogue." In *Handbook of World Families*, edited by Bert N. Adams and Jan Trost, 603–5. Thousand Oaks, CA: Sage, 2005.

Adams-Budde, Melissa, et al. "Examining the Literacy Histories of Doctoral Students in an Educational Studies Program through Surveys and Interviews: A Mixed Methods Study." *Journal of the Scholarship of Teaching and Learning* 14 (2014) 109–25.

Ainsworth, Mary S. "Infant-Mother Attachment." *American Psychologist* 34 (1979) 932–37.

Alexander, Mallika, et al. "Romance and Sex: Premarital Partnership Formation Among Young Women, and Men, Pune District, India." *Reproductive Health Matters* 14 (2006) 144–55.

Allendorf, Keera, and Dirgha Ghimire. "Determinants of Marital Quality in an Arranged Marriage Society." *Social Science Research* 42 (2013) 59–70.

Al Naser, Fahad. "Kuwait's Families." In *Handbook of World Families*, edited by Bert N. Adams and Jan Trost, 507–35. Thousand Oaks, CA: Sage, 2005.

Amaro, Fausto. "The Family in Portugal: Past and Present." In *Handbook of World Families*, edited by Bert N. Adams and Jan Trost, 330–46. Thousand Oaks, CA: Sage, 2005.

Applbaum, Kalman D. "Marriage with the Proper Stranger: Arranged Marriage in Metropolitan Japan." *Ethnology* 34 (1995) 37–52.

Arghode, Vishal. "Qualitative and Quantitative Research: Paradigmatic Differences." *Global Education Journal* 4 (2012) 155–63.

Aron, Arthur, et al. "Inclusion of Other in the Self Scale and the Structure of Interpersonal Closeness." *Journal of Personality and Social Psychology* 63 (1992) 596–612.

Azadarmaki, Taghi. "Families in Iran: The Contemporary Situation." In *Handbook of World Families*, edited by Bert N. Adams and Jan Trost, 467–85. Thousand Oaks, CA: Sage, 2005.

Barnes, Brendon R. "Using Mixed Methods in South African Psychological Research." *South African Journal of Psychology* 42 (2012) 463–75.

Bartholomew, Theodore T., and Jill R. Brown. "Mixed Methods, Culture, and Psychology: A Review of Mixed Methods in Culture-Specific Psychological Research." *International Perspectives in Psychology, Research, Practice, Consultation* 1 (2012) 177–90.

Batabyal, Amitrajeet A. "On the Likelihood of Finding the Right Partner in an Arranged Marriage." *Journal of Socio-Economics* 33 (2001) 273–80.

Boateng, Alice. "A Mixed Methods Analysis of Social Capital of Liberian Refugee Women in Ghana." *Journal of Sociology and Social Welfare* 36 (2009) 59–81.

Bose, Sunita, and Scott J. South. "Sex Composition of Children and Marital Disruption in India." *Journal of Marriage and Family* 65 (2003) 996–1006.

Bourque, Linda B., and Eve P. Fielder. *How to Conduct Self-Administered and Mail Surveys*. Thousand Oaks, CA: Sage, 2003.

Bowlby, John. *A Secure Base: Clinical Applications of Attachment Theory*. New York: Routledge, 2005.

———. *A Secure Base: Parent-Child Attachment and Healthy Human Development*. New York: Basic, 1988.

Bradbury, Thomas N., et al. "Research on the Nature and Determinants of Marital Satisfaction: A Decade in Review." *Journal of Marriage and Family* 62 (2000) 964–80.

Bradbury, Thomas N., and Benjamin R. Karney. *Intimate Relationships*. New York: Norton, 2010.

Bradley, Brent, and Susan M. Johnson. "Task Analysis of Couple and Family Change Events." In *Research Methods in Family Therapy*, edited by Douglas H. Sprenkle and Fred P. Piercy, 254–71. New York: Guilford, 2005.

Broderick, Carlfred B. *Marriage and the Family*. New Jersey: Prentice Hall, 1992.

Bronfenbrenner, Urie. *The Ecology of Human Development: Experiments by Nature and Design*. Cambridge: Harvard University Press, 1979.

Caldwell, J. C., et al. "The Causes of Marriage in South India." *Population Studies* 37 (1983) 343–61.

———. "The Determinants of Family Structure in Rural South India." *Journal of Marriage and Family* 46 (1984) 215–29.

Carroll, Jamuna. "Introduction." In *India: Opposing Viewpoints*, edited by Jamuna Carroll, 14–17. Detroit: Greenhaven, 2009.

Chacko, Elizabeth. "Marriage, Development, and the Status of Women in Kerala, India." *Gender and Development* 11 (2003) 52–59.

Chawla, Devika. "I Will Speak Out: Narratives of Resistance in Contemporary Indian Women's Discourses in Hindu Arranged Marriages." *Women and Language* 30 (2007) 5–19.

———. "Subjectivity and the 'Native' Ethnographer: Researcher Eligibility in an Ethnographic Study of Urban Indian Women in Hindu Arranged Marriages." *International Journal of Qualitative Methods* 5 (2006) 1–13.

Chekki, Dan A. "Family Values and Family Change." *Journal of Comparative Family Studies* 27 (1996) 409–13.

———. "Recent Directions in Family Research: India and North America." *Journal of Comparative Family Studies* 19 (1988) 171–86.

Chen, Chu Sheng, and Xiang Qian Zhang. "The Risk Recognition of Enterprise Creative Talents Based on Ecological System Theory." *Journal of Chemical and Pharmaceutical Research* 5 (2013) 118–23.

Chen, Yu-Hua, and Chin-Chun Yi. "Taiwan's Families." In *Handbook of World Families*, edited by Bert N. Adams and Jan Trost, 177–98. Thousand Oaks, CA: Sage, 2005.

Chojnacki, Joseph T., and W. Bruce Walsh. "Reliability and Concurrent Validity of the Sternberg Triangular Love Scale." *Psychological Report* 67 (1990) 219–24.

Coontz, Stephanie. *Marriage, a History: How Love Conquered Marriage*. New York: Penguin, 2005.

Corcoran, Kevin, and Joel Fischer. *Measures for Clinical Practice*. New York: Free Press, 2000.

Creswell, John W. *Qualitative Inquiry and Research Design: Choosing Among Five Approaches*. Thousand Oaks, CA: Sage, 2007.

————. *Research Design: Qualitative, Quantitative, and Mixed Methods Approaches*. Thousand Oaks, CA: Sage, 2009.

Cusack, Claire E., et al. "Components of Love and Relationship Satisfaction: Lesbians and Heterosexual Women." *Journal of Psychological Research* 17 (2012) 171–79.

D'Cruz, Premilla, and Shalini Bharat. "Beyond Joint and Nuclear: The Indian Family Revisited." *Journal of Comparative Family Studies* 32 (2001) 167–94.

De Vaus, David. "Australian Families." In *Handbook of World Families*, edited by Bert N. Adams and Jan Trost, 67–98. Thousand Oaks, CA: Sage, 2005.

Diamond, Gary M., et al. "Attachment-Based Family Therapy: Adherence and Differentiation." *Journal of Marital and Family Therapy* 33 (2007) 177–91.

Dumon, Wilfried. "Belgium's Families." In *Handbook of World Families*, edited by Bert N. Adams and Jan Trost, 215–34. Thousand Oaks, CA: Sage, 2005.

Dupree, W. Jared, et al. "Developing Culturally Competent Marriage and Family Therapists: Guidelines for Working with Asian Indian American Couples." *American Journal of Family Therapy* 41 (2013) 311–29.

Easton, Kristen L., et al. "Avoiding Common Pitfalls in Qualitative Data Collection and Transcription." *Qualitative Health Research* 10 (2000) 703–7.

Etcheverry, Paul E., et al. "Attachment and the Investment Model: Predictors of Relationship Commitment, Maintenance, and Persistence." *Personal Relationships* 20 (2012) 546–67.

————. "Predictors of Friend Approval for Romantic Relationships." *Personal Relationships* 20 (2013) 69–83.

Farrelly, Penny. "Choosing the Right Method for a Qualitative Study." *British Journal of School Nursing* 8 (2013) 42–44.

Faul, Franz, et al. "Statistical Power Analyses Using G*Power 3.1: Tests for Correlation and Regression Analyses." *Behavior Research Methods* 41 (2009) 1149–60.

Fincham, Frank D., and Thomas N. Bradbury. "The Assessment of Marital Quality: A Reevaluation." *Journal of Marriage and Family* 49 (1987) 797–809.

Fletcher, Garth J. O., et al. "The Measurement of Perceived Relationship Quality Components: A Confirmatory Factor Analysis Approach." *Personality and Social Psychology Bulletin* 26 (2000) 340–54.

Forsberg, Hannele. "Finland's Families." In *Handbook of World Families*, edited by Bert N. Adams and Jan Trost, 262–82. Thousand Oaks, CA: Sage, 2005.

Fuller, C. J., and Haripriya Narasimhan. "Companionate Marriage in India: The Changing Marriage System in a Middle-Class Brahman Subcaste." *Journal of Royal Anthropological Institute* 14 (2008) 736–54.

Ganguly-Scrase, Ruchira. "Paradoxes of Globalization, Liberalization, and Gender Equality: The Worldviews of Lower Middle Class in West Bengal, India." *Gender and Society* 17 (2003) 544–66.

Gopalakrishnan, Narayan, and Hurriet Babacan. "Ties that Bind: Marriage and Partner Choice in the Indian Community in Australia in a Transnational Context." *Global Studies in Culture and Power* 14 (2007) 507–26.

Gopalan, L. "Incest in India—How Safe are Our Daughters?" *MedIndia* (March 2009). http://www.medindia.net/news/indiaspecial/incest-in-indiahow-safe-are-our-daughters-49237-1.htm.

Gottman, John M. *The Marriage Clinic: A Scientifically Based Marital Therapy*. New York: Norton, 1999.

Gottman, John M., and Julie S. Gottman. "Gottman Method Couple Therapy." In *Clinical Handbook of Couple Therapy*, edited by Alan S. Gurman, 138–66. New York: Guilford, 2008.

Gould, Jay E. *Concise Handbook of Experimental Methods for the Behavioral and Biological Sciences*. Boca Raton, FL: CRC, 2002.

Guha, Ramachandra. *India After Gandhi: The History of the World's Largest Democracy*. New York: HarperCollins, 2007.

Hall, Scott S. "Implicit Theories of the Marital Institution." *Marriage and Family Review* 48 (2012) 1–19.

Harvey, Carol D. H. "Families in Canada." In *Handbook of World Families*, edited by Bert N. Adams and Jan Trost, 539–59. Thousand Oaks, CA: Sage, 2005.

Hazan, Cindy, and Lisa M. Diamond. "The Place of Attachment in Human Mating." *Review of General Psychology* 4 (2000) 186–204.

Heller, Patrice E., and Beatrice Wood. "The Influence of Religious and Ethnic Differences on Marital Intimacy: Intermarriage Versus Intramarriage." *Journal of Marital and Family Therapy* 26 (2000) 241–52.

Hendrick, Clyde, and Susan S. Hendrick. "Research on Love: Does it Measure Up?" *Journal of Personality and Social Psychology* 56 (1989) 784–94.

Hendrick, Susan S. "A Generic Measure of Relationship Satisfaction." *Journal of Marriage and Family* 50 (1988) 93–98.

———. "Relationship Assessment Scale (RAS)." In *Measures for Clinical Practice: A Source Book*, edited by Kevin Corcoran and Joel Fischer, 171–72. New York: Free Press, 2000.

Hendrick, Susan S., et al. "The Relationship Assessment Scale." *Journal of Social and Personal Relationships* 15 (1998) 137–42.

Herring, Melissa, and Nadine J. Kaslow. "Depression and Attachment in Families: A Child-Focused Perspective." *Family Process* 41 (2002) 494–518.

Hill, Clara E. "Qualitative Research." In *Evidence Based Practices in Mental Health: Debate and Dialogue on the Fundamental Questions*, edited by John C. Norcross et al., 74–81. Washington, DC: APA, 2006.

Hill, Jonathan, et al. "The Ecology of Attachment in the Family." *Family Process* 42 (2003) 205–21.

Hoe, Juanita, and Zoe Hoare. "Understanding Quantitative Research: Part 1." *Nursing Standard* 27 (2012) 52–57.

Hoelter, Lynette F., et al. "Social Change, Premarital Nonfamily Experiences, and Marital Dynamics." *Journal of Marriage and Family* 66 (2004) 1131–51.

Howell, David C. *Statistical Methods for Psychology*. Belmont, CA: Wadsworth, 2010.

Hughes, Daniel A. "An Attachment-Based Treatment of Maltreated Children and Young People." *Attachment and Development* 6 (2004) 263–78.

———. *Attachment-Focused Family Therapy*. New York: Norton, 2007.

———. *Attachment-Focused Parenting: Effective Strategies to Care for Children*. New York: Norton, 2009.

Husserl, Edmund. *Cartesian Meditations: An Introduction to Phenomenology.* Translated by Dorion Cairns. The Hague, Netherlands: Martinus Nijhoff, 1950/1960.

———. *The Idea of Phenomenology.* Translated by L. Hardy. Dordrecht, Netherlands: Kluwer Academic, 1950/1999.

Hutchinson, Sally A., et al. "Benefits of Participating in Research Interviews." *Image: Journal of Nursing Scholarship* 26 (1994) 161–64.

Ireland, Molly E., et al. "Language Style Matching Predicts Relationship Initiation and Stability." *Psychological Science* 22 (2010) 39–44.

Jacobson, Doranne. "Social Systems." In *India: A Country Study*, edited by James Heitzman and Robert L. Worden, 231–94. Washington, DC: Library of Congress, 1996.

Jelin, Elizabeth. "The Family in Argentina: Modernity, Economic Crisis, and Politics." In *Handbook of World Families*, edited by Bert N. Adams and Jan Trost, 391–413. Thousand Oaks, CA: Sage, 2005.

Johnson, Susan M. "The Revolution in Couple Therapy: A Practitioner-Scientist Perspective." *Journal of Marital and Family Therapy* 29 (2003) 365–84.

Joshi, Vijay. "Economic Resurgence, Lopsided Reform and Jobless Growth." In *Diversity and Change in Modern India: Economic, Social and Political Approaches*, edited by Anthony F. Heath and Roger Jeffery, 73–106. New York: Oxford University Press, 2010.

Katz, Ruth, and Yoav Lavee. "Families in Israel." In *Handbook of World Families*, edited by Bert N. Adams and Jan Trost, 486–506. Thousand Oaks, CA: Sage, 2005.

Keiley, Margaret K. "Attachment and Affect Regulation: A Framework for Family Treatment of Conduct Disorder." *Family Process* 41 (2002) 477–93.

Khalakdina, Margaret. *Human Development in the Indian Context: A Socio-Cultural Focus.* New Delhi: Sage, 2008.

Khatri, A. A. "The Adaptive Extended Family in India Today." *Journal of Marriage and Family* 37 (1975) 633–42.

Klein, Thomas, and Bernhard Nauck. "Families in Germany." In *Handbook of World Families*, edited by Bert N. Adams and Jan Trost, 283–312. Thousand Oaks, CA: Sage, 2005.

Klumb, Petra, et al. "Division of Labor in German Dual-Earner Families: Testing Equity Theoretical Hypotheses." *Journal of Marriage and Family* 68 (2006) 870–82.

Lawrence, Erika, et al. "The Relationship Quality Interview: Evidence of Reliability, Convergent and Divergent Validity, and Incremental Utility." *Psychological Assessment* 23 (2011) 44–63.

LeCompte, Margaret D., and Jean J. Schensul. *Analysis and Interpretation of Ethnographic Data: A Mixed Methods Approach.* Lanham, MD: AltaMira, 2013.

Lee, Kwang-Kyu. "South Korean Families." In *Handbook of World Families*, edited by Bert N. Adams and Jan Trost, 167–76. Thousand Oaks, CA: Sage, 2005.

Leon, Kim, and Deborah B. Jacobvitz. "Relationships Between Adult Attachment Representations and Family Ritual Quality: A Prospective, Longitudinal Study." *Family Process* 42 (2003) 419–32.

Macher, Silvia. "Social Interdependence in Close Relationships: The Actor-Partner-Interdependence-Investment Model (API-IM)." *European Journal of Social Psychology* 43 (2013) 84–96.

Madathil, Jayamala, and James M. Benshoff. "Importance of Marital Characteristics and Marital Satisfaction: A Comparison of Asian Indians in Arranged Marriages and Americans in Marriages of Choice." *The Family Journal* 16 (2008) 222–30.

Madey, Scott F., and Lindsey Rodgers. "The Effect of Attachment and Sternberg's Triangular Theory of Love on Relationship Satisfaction." *Individual Differences Research* 7 (2009) 76–84.

Malinen, Kaisa, et al. "Happy Spouses, Happy Parents? Family Relationships Among Finnish and Dutch Dual Earners." *Journal of Marriage and Family* 72 (2010) 293–306.

Marshall, Catherine, and Gretchen B. Rossman. *Designing Qualitative Research.* Thousand Oaks, CA: Sage, 1999.

Mason, Mark. "Sample Size and Saturation in PhD Studies Using Qualitative Interviews." *Forum: Qualitative Social Research* 11 (September 2010). http://nbn-resolving.de/urn:nbn:de:0114-fqs100387.

Massengale, Kelley, et al. "Exploration of Undergraduate Preservice Teachers' Experiences Learning Advocacy: A Mixed-Methods Study." *Journal of the Scholarship of Teaching and Learning* 14 (2014) 75–92.

Mburugu, Edward K., and Bert N. Adams. "Families in Kenya." In *Handbook of World Families,* edited by Bert N. Adams and Jan Trost, 3–24. Thousand Oaks, CA: Sage, 2005.

McLaren, Lindsay, and Penelope Hawe. "Ecological Perspectives in Health Research." *Journal of Epidemiology and Community Health* 59 (2005) 6–14.

McWilliams, Nancy. *Psychoanalytic Diagnosis.* New York: Guilford, 2011.

Medora, Nilufer P. "Strengths and Challenges in the Indian Family." *Marriage and Family Review* 41 (2007) 165–93.

Mikulincer, Mario, et al. "Attachment Security in Couple Relationships: A Systemic Model and Its Implications for Family Dynamics." *Family Process* 41 (2002) 405–34.

Mishra, Anurag, et al. "Men's Attitudes on Gender Equality and Their Contraceptive Use in Uttar Pradesh India." *Reproductive Health* 11 (2014) 1–13.

Modo, Innocent Victor Ogo. "Nigerian Families." In *Handbook of World Families,* edited by Bert N. Adams and Jan Trost, 25–46. Thousand Oaks, CA: Sage, 2005.

Moore, Kathleen A., et al. "Are Married Couples Happier in Their Relationships than Cohabiting Couples? Intimacy and Relationship Factors." *Sexual and Relationship Therapy* 16 (2001) 35–45.

Moustakas, Clark. *Phenomenological Research Methods.* Thousand Oaks, CA: Sage, 1994.

Mozny, Ivo, and Tomas Katrnak. "The Czech Family." In *Handbook of World Families,* edited by Bert N. Adams and Jan Trost, 235–61. Thousand Oaks, CA: Sage, 2005.

Musick, Kelly, and Larry Bumpass. "Reexamining the Case for Marriage: Union Formation and Changes in Well-Being." *Journal of Marriage and Family* 74 (2012) 1–18.

Myers, Jane E., et al. "Marriage Satisfaction and Wellness in India and the United States: A Preliminary Comparison of Arranged Marriages and Marriages of Choice." *Journal of Counseling and D* 83 (2005) 183–90.

Natrajan, Balmurli. "Caste, Class, and Community in India: An Ethnographic Approach." *Ethnology* 44 (2005) 227–41.

Natrajan, Rajeswari, and Volker Thomas. "Need for Family Therapy Services for Middle-Class Families in India." *Contemporary Family Therapy* 24 (2002) 483–503.

Nauck, Bernhard, and Daniela Klaus. "Families in Turkey." In *Handbook of World Families,* edited by Bert N. Adams and Jan Trost, 364–88. Thousand Oaks, CA: Sage, 2005.

Neal, Jennifer Watling, and Zachary P. Neal. "Nested or Networked? Future Directions for Ecological Systems Theory." *Social Development* 22 (2013) 722–37.

Nelson, Thorana S., and David D. Allred. "Survey Research in Marriage and Family Therapy." In *Research Methods in Family Therapy*, edited by Douglas H. Sprenkle and Fred P. Piercy, 211–37. New York: Guilford, 2005.

Netting, Nancy S. "Marital Ideoscapes in 21st Century India: Creative Combinations of Love and Responsibilities." *Journal of Family Issues* 31 (2010) 707–26.

Ng, Ting Kin, and Christopher H. K. Cheng. "The Effects of Intimacy, Passion, and Commitment on Satisfaction in Romantic Relationships Among Hong Kong Chinese People." *Journal of Psychology in Chinese Societies* 11 (2010) 123–46.

Nolte, Sandra et al. "Absence of Social Desirability Bias in the Evaluation of Chronic Disease Self-Management Interventions." *Health and Quality of Life Outcomes* 11 (2013) 1–9.

Overbreek, Geertjan, et al. "Brief Report: Intimacy, Passion, and Commitment in Romantic Relationships—Validation of a 'Triangular Love Scale' for Adolescents." *Journal of Adolescence* 30 (2007) 523–28.

Panayiotou, Georgia. "Love, Commitment, and Response to Conflict Among Cypriot Dating Couples: Two Models, One Relationship." *International Journal of Psychology* 40 (2005) 108–17.

Parra-Cardona, Jose Ruben, et al. "'Changing for My Kid': Fatherhood Experiences of Mexican-Origin Teen Fathers Involved in the Justice System." *Journal of Marital and Family Therapy* 34 (2008) 369–87.

Philips, Amali. "Gendering Color: Identity, Femininity and Marriage in Kerala." *Anthropologica* 46 (2004) 253–72.

Pimentel, Ellen Efron. "Just How Do I love Thee? Marital Relations in Urban China." *Journal of Marriage and Family* 62 (2000) 32–47.

Pistole, M. Carole, et al. "Commitment Predictors: Long-Distance Versus Geographically Close Relationships." *Journal of Counseling and Development* 88 (2010) 146–53.

Pratto, Felicia, and Angela Walker. "The Bases of Gendered Power." In *The Psychology of Gender*, edited by Alice H. Eagly et al., 242–68. New York: Guilford, 2004.

Purkayastha, Bandana, et al. "The Study of Gender in India: A Partial Review." *Gender and Society* 17 (2003) 503–24.

Ram, Malathi, and Rebeca Wong. "Covariates of Household Extension in Rural India: Change Over Time." *Journal of Marriage and Family* 56 (1994) 853–64.

Rask, Mikael, et al. "Validity and Reliability of a Swedish Version of the Relationship Assessment Scale (RAS): A Pilot Study." *Canadian Journal of Cardiovascular Nursing* 20 (2010) 16–21.

Rea, Louis M., and Richard A. Parker. *Designing and Conducting Survey Research: A Comprehensive Guide*. San Francisco, CA: Jossey-Bass, 2005.

Reitz, O. Ed, and Mary Ann Anderson. "A Comparison of Survey Methods in Studies of the Nurse Workforce." *Nurse Researcher* 20 (2013) 22–27.

Renshaw, Keith D., et al. "The Utility of the Relationship Assessment Scale in Multiple Types of Relationships." *Journal of Social and Personal Relationships* 28 (2010) 435–47.

Rhyne, Darla. "Bases of Marital Satisfaction Among Men and Women." *Journal of Marriage and Family* 43 (1981) 941–55.

Richter, Rudolf, and Sandra Kytir. "Families in Austria." In *Handbook of World Families*, edited by Bert N. Adams and Jan Trost, 201–14. Thousand Oaks, CA: Sage, 2005.

Ridgeway, Cecilia L., and Chris Bourg. "Gender as Status: An Expectation States Theory Approach." In *The Psychology of Gender*, edited by Alice H. Eagly et al., 217–41. New York: Guilford, 2004.

Rodrigues, David, and Diniz Lopes. "The Investment Model Scale (IMS): Further Studies on Construct Validation and Development of a Shorter Version (IMS-S)." *Journal of General Psychology* 140 (2013) 16–28.

Roulston, Kathryn, et al. "Learning to Interview in the Social Sciences." *Qualitative Inquiry* 9 (2003) 643–68.

Rubin, Zick. "Measurement of Romantic Love." *Journal of Personality and Social Psychology* 16 (1970) 265–73.

Rusbult, Caryl E., et al. "The Investment Model Scale: Measuring Commitment Level, Satisfaction Level, Quality of Alternatives, and Investment Size." *Personal Relationships* 5 (1998) 357–91.

Salvatore, Jessica E., et al. "Recovering from Conflict in Romantic Relationships: A Developmental Perspective." *Psychological Science* 22 (2011) 376–383.

Sandhya, Shaifali. "The Social Context of Marital Happiness in Urban Indian Couples: Interplay of Intimacy and Conflict." *Journal of Marital and Family Therapy* 35 (2009) 74–96.

Sayre, Julia B., et al. "An Outsider in My Own Home: Attachment Injury in Stepcouple Relationships." *Journal of Marital and Family Therapy* 36 (2010) 403–15.

Schumm, Walter R., et al. "Concurrent and Discriminant Validity of the Kansas Marital Satisfaction Scale." *Journal of Marriage and Family* 48 (1986) 381–87.

Seidman, Irving. *Interviewing as Qualitative Research: A Guide for Researchers in Education and the Social Sciences*. New York: Teachers College, 2006.

Settles, Barbara H. "U.S. Families." In *Handbook of World Families*, edited by Bert N. Adams and Jan Trost, 560–601. Thousand Oaks, CA: Sage, 2005.

Sheng, Xuewen. "Chinese Families." In *Handbook of World Families*, edited by Bert N. Adams and Jan Trost, 99–128. Thousand Oaks, CA: Sage, 2005.

Shenton, Andrew K. "Strategies for Ensuring Trustworthiness in Qualitative Research Projects." *Education for Information* 22 (2004) 63–75.

Shukla, Rakesh. "The Dowry and Cruelty Law Protects Women and is Constitutional." In *India: Opposing Viewpoints*, edited by Jamuna Carroll, 118–25. Detroit: Greenhaven, 2009.

Singh, J. P. "The Contemporary Indian Family." In *Handbook of World Families*, edited by Bert N. Adams and Jan Trost, 129–66. Thousand Oaks, CA: Sage, 2005.

Slatcher, Richard B., and James W. Pennebaker. "How Do I Love Thee? Let Me Count the Words: The Social Effects of Expressive Writing." *Psychological Science* 17 (2006) 660–64.

Spanier, Graham B. "Measuring Dyadic Adjustment: New Scales for Assessing the Quality of Marriage and Similar Dyads." *Journal of Marriage and Family* 38 (1976) 15–28.

Speziale, Helen J. Streubert, and Dona Rinaldi Carpenter. *Qualitative Research in Nursing: Advancing the Humanistic Imperative*. Philadelphia: Lippincott Williams & Wilkins, 2007.

Sprenkle, Douglas H., and Fred P. Piercy. "Pluralism, Diversity, and Sophistication in Family Therapy Research." In *Research Methods in Family Therapy*, edited by Douglas H. Sprenkle and Fred P. Piercy, 3–18. New York: Guilford, 2005.

Srinivasan, Padma, and Gary R. Lee. "The Dowry System in Northern India: Women's Attitudes and Social Change." *Journal of Marriage and Family* 66 (2004) 1108–17.

Sternberg, Robert J. "Construct Validation of a Triangular Love Scale." *European Journal of Social Psychology* 27 (1997) 313–35.

———. "A Triangular Theory of Love." *Psychological Review* 93 (1986) 119–35.

———. "Triangular Theory of Love Scales." In *Conceptualizing and Measuring "Healthy Marriages" for Empirical Research and Evaluation Studies: A Compendium of Measures—Part II*. Washington, DC: Child Trends, 2003. https://www.childtrends.org/wp-content/uploads/2013/09/Healthy-Marriages-Part-II.pdf.

Sweetman, Caroline. "Editorial." *Gender Development* 11 (2003) 2–7.

Szalavitz, Maia, and Bruce D. Perry. *Born for Love: Why Empathy is Essential—and Endangered*. New York: Harper Collins, 2010.

Terrell, Steven R. "Mixed-Methods Research Methodologies." *The Qualitative Report* 17 (2012) 254–80.

Toth, Olga, and Peter Somlai. "Families in Hungary." In *Handbook of World Families*, edited by Bert N. Adams and Jan Trost, 313–29. Thousand Oaks, CA: Sage, 2005.

Trost, Jan, and Irene Levin. "Scandinavian Families." In *Handbook of World Families*, edited by Bert N. Adams and Jan Trost, 347–63. Thousand Oaks, CA: Sage, 2005.

Vaid, Divya, and Anthony Heath. "Unequal Opportunities: Class, Caste and Social Mobility." In *Diversity and Change in Modern India: Economic, Social and Political Approaches*, edited by Anthony F. Heath and Roger Jeffery, 129–64. New York: Oxford University Press, 2010.

Vanderdrift, Laura E., et al. "Commitment in Friends with Benefits Relationships: Implications for Relational and Safe-Sex Outcomes." *Personal Relationships* 19 (2012) 1–13.

Vanita, Ruth. "The Self is Not Gendered: Sulabha's Debate with King Janaka." *NWSA Journal* 15 (2003) 76–93.

Venkatesh, Viswanath, et al. "Bridging the Qualitative–Quantitative Divide: Guidelines for Conducting Mixed Methods Research in Information Systems." *MIS Quarterly* 37 (2013) 21–54.

Wampler, Karen S., et al. "The Adult Attachment Interview and Observed Couple Interaction: Implications for an Intergenerational Perspective on Couple Therapy." *Family Process* 42 (2003) 497–515.

White, Kathleen M., et al. "Intimacy Maturity and its Correlates in Young Married Couples." *Journal of Personality and Social Psychology* 50 (1986) 152–162.

Wisdom, Jennifer P., et al. "Methodological Reporting in Qualitative, Quantitative, and Mixed Methods Health Services Research Articles." *Health Services Research* 47 (2012) 721–45.

Xiaohe, Xu, and Martin King Whyte. "Love Matches and Arranged Matches: A Chinese Replication." *Journal of Marriage and Family* 52 (1990) 709–22.

Yelsma, Paul, and Kuriakose Athappilly. "Marital Satisfaction and Communication Practices: Comparisons Among Indian and American Couples." *Journal of Comparative Family Studies* 19 (1988) 37–54.

Zaidi, Arshia U., and Muhammad Shuraydi. "Perceptions of Arranged Marriages by Young Pakistani Muslim Women Living in a Western Society." *Journal of Comparative Family Studies* 33 (2002) 495–514.

Zang, Xiaowei. "Gender and Ethnic Variation in Arranged Marriages in a Chinese City." *Journal of Family Issues* 29 (2008) 615–38.

Zhang, Yuping, et al. "Do Mothers in Rural China Practice Gender Equality in Educational Aspirations for Their Children?" *Comparative Education Review* 51 (2007) 131–57.

BIBLIOGRAPHY

Ziehl, Susan C. "Families in South Africa." In *Handbook of World Families*, edited by Bert N. Adams and Jan Trost, 47–63. Thousand Oaks, CA: Sage, 2005.

Zuo, Jiping. "Women's Liberation and Gender Obligation Equality in Urban China: Work/Family Experiences of Married Individuals in the 1950s." *Science and Society* 77 (2013) 98–125.